For all the women who have been called "Jezebel"
or had their gender used against them.

"Behold, I am making all things new." (Revelation 21:5)

TABLE OF CONTENTS

Infomercial

Hi. I'm Robyn, a minister and biblical scholar from Melbourne, Australia. This book provides a brief introduction to the last book in the Bible called the Apocalypse, or Revelation. I think of Revelation as the weird cousin in the Bible—the one you have to invite to family events but would rather not spend much time with. It is one of those biblical books that Christians either ignore or get a little bit too obsessed with (you know the people I mean).

I became curious about Revelation as a teenager when I began hanging out with evangelical Christians. They quoted this text as if its meaning were obvious and we could directly map its contents onto our contemporary world. Yet, when I read it, what they saw as obvious didn't seem very obvious to me at all. It was strange and confusing. Nothing in my mainstream church background had prepared me to read Revelation: we didn't really talk about it. So, when I went to seminary, I jumped at the chance to take a class on Revelation. And thus began my love-hate-love affair with this book.

A few years before I started seminary, seventy-six people tragically died after a prolonged siege at the Mount Carmel Compound in Waco, Texas. As a South-African-born Australian migrant, the events at Waco were the first thing I learned about Texas, cementing in my mind the idea that religion gets a little wacky in certain parts of America. (Sorry, Texans—I have since lived in the U.S. and now know that you have great food and some pretty cool cities!)

During the media coverage of the Waco siege much was written about the cult known as the Branch Davidians. It is tempting to dismiss this group as brainwashed extremists who were duped by their clever but troubled leader, David Koresh, but we cannot do so too quickly. It is now well established that Koresh's main biblical focus was Revelation: he described the community as "students of the seven seals" and proclaimed himself the Lamb of God who could open the seven seals and therefore interpret the prophecy.[1] (The idea that a human leader is Revelation's Lamb is unique to the Davidians.) The Davidian community interpreted the book of Revelation literally and, therefore, had prepared themselves for a literal holy war in anticipation of Christ's imminent second coming. They were highly dualistic, seeing themselves as "the righteous" and identifying US government officials as agents of the evil empire. In such a worldview, violence is normalized and necessary for the end to come, martyrdom becomes the ultimate expression of faithfulness, and marginalized groups claim the status of a righteous minority who are at war with an evil majority. Alarmingly, their apocalyptic worldview—which set them against the world—is all too common and has been found among readers of Revelation throughout history.[2]

---

[1] During the siege, Koresh (real name: Vernon Howell) discussed his interpretation of Revelation with FBI negotiators. He was also writing an interpretation of Revelation that remains unfinished. One of the transcripts of Koresh's conversations with FBI agents can be viewed at Frontline, "Waco: The Inside Story," October 17, 1995, https://www.pbs.org/wgbh/pages/frontline/waco/bookofrevel.html.

[2] A similar, but much smaller scale event occurred in Australia in December 2022, when several police were killed investigating a group on a remote Queensland property. Those involved have been described as "fundamentalist Christian terrorists," who were deeply apocalyptic and saw themselves as God's righteous ones fighting a government of "monsters and demons." It doesn't just happen in the U.S. See Kym Agius, "Queensland police say Wieambilla shooting was 'a religiously motivated terrorist attack,'" ABC News, February 16, 2023, https://www.abc.net.au/news/2023-02-16/wieambilla-police-shooting-religious-terrorist-attack/101983612.

I start by recalling the events at Waco because it is just one among many possible examples of how dangerous it can be to read books like Revelation in a literalistic way. The vivid imagery and violence of Revelation, when seen as normative (or worse, divinely mandated) can and has been used to justify earthly violence. Throughout history, Revelation's visions of the end times have been interpreted as predicting a period of tribulation, judgment, and even the rapture.[3] The number of the beast (666) has been associated with any number of world leaders as a way of rejecting their views and institutions. And these interpretations are not confined to the past. A quick internet search uncovers a myriad of websites and social media accounts dedicated to tracking how the prophecies of Revelation are being fulfilled in the contemporary world. Beliefs like these, which anticipate a literal fulfillment of the visions and events described in Revelation, are part of the problematic legacy of this text. One of our goals here is to bust open such myths and look at what is—and is not—actually in Revelation. (Spoiler alert: there is no rapture in Revelation.)

Among the reasons Revelation is so confusing and prone to being misinterpreted is that it is highly symbolic and non-linear, and it contains coded references to a bunch of things that probably made some sense in the first century CE, but are not part of our everyday language and worldview today. Therefore, we need to situate Revelation in its original context—the first century CE—to unpack the way it works. We need to consider the type of literature it is, and then we need to think about how on earth we interpret it for the modern world. That is our goal in the pages ahead. I encourage you to have a Bible at hand, as this book is best read with the text of Revelation open.

---

[3] "The rapture" refers to a belief that when Jesus returns at the end of time, believers who are alive will be lifted up from the earth to meet him in the sky. It is based on a literal interpretation of 1 Thessalonians 4:17 which says "we who are alive, who are left, will be caught up in the clouds together with them to meet the Lord in the air."

We will situate Revelation in its context as a piece of Christian resistance literature written to help first-century Christ followers navigate life within the Roman Empire. By looking at what images and symbols meant in that ancient time and place, we will discover that Revelation is a highly political, but also deeply theological, text. It offers us a profound way to think about evil as something found in structures and systems, and to ponder what an ethical response to such evil might be. It is also just a little bit weird, which, in my opinion, makes our journey through its pages that much more interesting.

CHAPTER ONE

Revelation from 30,000 Feet

Chances are you know about the book of Revelation even if you have never read it. This is the biblical book that describes the great Whore of Babylon, reinvents "wicked" Jezebel from the Hebrew Bible,[1] tells of the archangel Michael with his heavenly army, describes a group of 144,000 saved male virgins, and depicts the four horsemen of the apocalypse. It also vividly portrays a hell-like place made of sulfur and fire, and it offers up movie-like scenes of apocalyptic catastrophe, where the world is destroyed multiple times over. And this is all before we get to that famous number: 666. These images and symbols have entered our popular imagination through art, literature, movies, songs, and conspiracy theories; and in many cases, they have taken on a life of their own, imbued with meanings far removed from the original text.

Images and phrases from Revelation also permeate Christian worship. Liturgies and hymns are infused with language from Revelation,

---

[1] I am using Hebrew Bible to refer to the collection of texts Christians often call the Old Testament. Both terms have their problems, but my choice to refer to the Old Testament as Hebrew Bible throughout is to remind us that Revelation draws upon Jewish texts, is deeply connected to a Jewish tradition, and reflects a worldview typical of Judaism in its period.

often quoting directly from the text: Almighty, alpha and omega, the glassy sea, casting our crowns, Jesus as shining or as slaughtered Lamb, the tree of life, water of life, and New Jerusalem, to give but a few examples. At funerals one might hear the lines that God "will wipe every tear from their eye," or "there will be no more mourning," both of which come from Revelation (7:17; 21:4).[2] This book is strangely familiar and yet simultaneously unfamiliar, and part of our task here is to strip away the history of interpretation that sometimes obscures the text and read it again in its first-century setting.

Amidst all the drama and symbolism of Revelation is a message to anxious ancient Christian communities which tells them that God sees their pain and struggle. God is, despite appearances, all-powerful and reigning in heaven, and God is doing something about the injustice on earth. The communities' job as followers of the Lamb is to worship, witness, and wait.

Covering the Basics

A "Revelation"

The book of Revelation is just that—a revelation from God to John to let him know "what must happen soon" (1:1). That line might make us think this text is about predicting the future, but it's not. Mostly, it's about the present and how to live in the world. The first thing to note is that John recounts just one Revelation. (Please don't call it the book of Revelations—there is no final 's'!) According to John, this vision, or "revelation", was given to him by God, mediated through Jesus and an angel.

The word we translate as "revelation" or "apocalypse" is *apocalypsis* in Greek, which means something hidden that is uncovered, or something secret that is disclosed. Revelation is the only full apocalypse in

---

[2] Translations are my own throughout.

the Bible, although we have apocalyptic-style writing in other texts, like Ezekiel, Daniel 7–10, Isaiah 6, and Mark 13. Apocalypses often narrate visionary experiences and use symbolism to communicate deep and difficult truths about God and the world.

We might think of an apocalypse in this way: imagine walking into a darkened room. There is a large window, but it's covered by a thick curtain and hardly any light filters through. You can't see what is outside and, since the room is dark, you cannot see anything in the room clearly either. Then someone opens the curtain and through the window you can now see a vista of great beauty. Sunlight streams into the room and changes the space you stand in, illuminating what you could not see clearly before. With the curtain open, you gain a sense of perspective and become aware of your location in the wider context of the world out there. The sunlight also helps you see the space you are standing in far better.

This is how apocalyptic literature functions. It gives us a glimpse of something previously hidden that, when revealed, transforms the world and the way we see it. It's not a crystal ball to gaze into the future Harry Potter style (that's divination). It is about revealing something that has always been there but has previously been hidden from view.

Before we talk more about what is revealed in Revelation, it might be helpful to correct some popular misconceptions about it. The book of Revelation

- is *not* a timeline of current world events that allows us to predict end time events;
- is *not* a code for identifying the antichrist;
- does *not* include a rapture;
- is *not* about escaping this world by going up to heaven (God recreates this world);
- does *not* predict that the number 666 refers to barcodes, microchips, vaccines, or _____ (insert your favorite conspiracy theory here).

What Is Revealed?

The thing being revealed in Revelation is primarily God and what God is doing in relation to the world. First and foremost, John wants his readers to know that God and Jesus are reigning in heaven and are in total control. The world might *feel* like it's going to hell in a hand-basket, but that's because God has already thrown evil (personified as the Dragon and his evil beasts) out of the heavenly realm, and they are roaming the earth, stirring up trouble and hurting the people of God. These monsters, and their followers, are about to be reminded who is really in charge. John tells this part of the story in multiple, overlapping ways.

What unfolds is a series of dramatic judgments of the earth and injustice. Breaking up the scenes of earthly drama are visions that take us back to the heavenly realm, where the followers of Jesus are encouraged when they see the saints already celebrating in heaven with God—this is a glimpse of their future life and the fulfilment of God's promises.

A simple outline of Revelation will help guide our reading. The book comprises

- a vision of Christ and his messages to the churches (1:1–3:22);
- a vision of God and the Lamb reigning in the heavenly throne room (4:1–5:14);
- sevenfold judgments of God (6:1–16:21);
- the judgment of Babylon/Rome and its monsters (17:1–20:15);
- re-creation: a new Heaven and a new Earth (21:1–22:21).

You can see that the middle section forms the bulk of the text, with its repeated series of seven judgments that come from God's throne down to earth (chapters 6–16). These judgments can leave the reader feeling overwhelmed by the violence depicted, an issue we will talk about later.

Authorship: Who Is John?

There are many theories about who John, the author of Revelation, might be. The author calls himself "John" four times (1:1, 4, 9; 22:8). But which John? The short answer is that we don't know. Theories about the identity of this author include the following: he was the apostle John, son of Zebedee, who is mentioned as a follower of Jesus in the Gospels (some think he wrote John's Gospel[3]); he was a church elder called John, whom some associate with the "beloved disciple" in John's Gospel; he possibly used the name John as a pseudonym. There is no strong evidence for any particular one of these theories, and it might be best to think of Revelation's John as a prophetic leader in the early Christian community who was active in Asia Minor. After all, this is who he tells us he is.

His name and actual identity aside, there are several details "John" mentions that tell us some interesting things about him. He is a "servant" of God and someone who witnesses to what God has revealed to him. Witnessing is really important in Revelation. The first description of Jesus is as a "faithful witness" (1:5), so those who want to be like Jesus need to witness like him.

John also describes himself as the audience's "brother" (1:9) using familial language typical of early Christianity. In doing so, he is appealing to what they have in common as believers, suggesting that not all of these Christian communities know him that well or agree with him. He claims this sibling status precisely because he has shared in their suffering and in their ministry as a witness to the word of God and to Jesus. It is an ancient version of an apostolic résumé: Look, I've also suffered for testifying about Jesus. I'm legit!

---

[3] To find out more about the authorship of John's Gospel, see *John for Normal People: A Guide through the Depth & Drama of the Fourth Gospel* by Jennifer Garcia Bashaw (Harleysville, PA: The Bible for Normal People, 2023).

John's identity as a prophet is equally important. He calls the words he writes "the prophecy" (1:3) and portrays himself, in the manner of Ezekiel and other biblical prophets, as someone who is "in the Spirit" (1:10), who receives visions, and who conveys God's direct words to the community. In a later scene, an angel tells John to eat a little scroll, which is as sweet as honey in his mouth but bitter in his belly (10:1–11). It's a total riff on Ezekiel 3, where the prophet Ezekiel also eats a honey-tasting scroll that symbolizes the sweet words of God, which he then prophesies to the people. Not that they listen, but that's another story. John imagines himself in this tradition,[4] as one of God's prophets and therefore someone speaking God's words. It is a reminder that he is Jewish and steeped in the Hebrew Bible. It is also a way of establishing his authority and his divine commission.

Audience: Who Is John Writing To?

John claims to write from Patmos (1:9), a Greek island off the coast of modern-day Turkey, to seven Christian communities in Asia Minor (Turkey): Ephesus, Smyrna, Pergamum, Thyatira, Sardis, Philadelphia, and Laodicea. He has a particular message for each of these churches, which, he asserts, is from the risen Jesus (1:4–5, 11; 2:1, 8, 12, 18; 3:1, 7, 14). There may well have been Christian communities in these seven towns, but the number seven also functions symbolically. Seven is the number of completeness or perfection, so symbolically, John writes to the whole Christ-believing church and these messages have universal appeal.

---

[4] The "tradition" I refer to here is the prophetic literature of the Hebrew Bible that begins to show traits of later apocalyptic literature. The vision of God's throne in Isaiah 6 and the visions in Ezekiel 1–3 are classic examples of this proto-apocalyptic literature. Zechariah is also another important prototype for Revelation and other Second Temple Jewish apocalyptic literature; it is also where John derives the idea of horsemen, a measuring line, lampstands, and a restored Jerusalem.

The location of the seven churches in Asia Minor is significant. In the late first century CE, when John writes, Asia Minor was under Roman rule. These were colonized peoples. They had to navigate holding on to local customs and practices while also meeting the demands of the Roman Empire, to whom they paid taxes and whose propaganda and power were everywhere. Members of these communities who were ethnically Jewish were also dispersed people—Jews living in the diaspora at some distance from Israel. They may have included people who had fled from the war that destroyed Jerusalem in 70 CE (I'll come back to this later). These Christian communities were generally not very powerful, influential, or even wealthy. They lived at the mercy of the empire and under the political whims of others far more powerful than themselves. The people John writes to are not only politically powerless; they are also the minority, at least in terms of their religion. They lived within a dominant culture that held different beliefs and worshiped different gods.

Was there Persecution?

Despite all that I have just mentioned, we have no historical evidence for widespread, systematic persecution of Christians in the last half of the first century CE. It is possible, however, that there was local and sporadic violence toward Christians, as well as economic and social pressures due to being followers of Jesus. In the message to Pergamum, for example, a member of the community called Antipas has been killed (2:13). We don't know why Antipas died, but he is called a "faithful witness" like Jesus, so we can assume it had something to do with his faith and witnessing. Other congregational messages suggest that there was also a very high degree of conflict between Jews and Christians, although we should not think of these as distinct groups yet; rather, John may have been referring to conflict between Jews who had come to believe Jesus was the expected Messiah and those who had not. As you can imagine, this might have caused a bit of a disturbance within synagogue communities.

We shall see that John's imagery is deeply influenced by the Hebrew Bible. Given how prevalent Hebrew Bible imagery is in Revelation, it is also possible that part of the persecution he mentions is that experienced by Jews, particularly during the Roman siege of Jerusalem (66–70 CE). This siege lasted many years before finally resulting in the destruction of the temple by the Roman army and the death, captivity, and dispersion of hundreds of thousands of Jews. We will see that this experience is reflected at numerous points in the text of Revelation.

Does persecution or war explain why John was on the island of Patmos? It is unclear. The traditional interpretation has been that John was exiled to Patmos as punishment for preaching about Jesus. While I have already suggested that Christians were not systematically singled out for persecution at this time, the Roman Empire definitely had a low tolerance for any kind of subversive teaching or activity that caused controversy. If John was arrested for preaching about Jesus in a way that challenged the empire, then the fact that he was banished, rather than sentenced to death or imprisonment, suggests he was a citizen with reasonable status. John simply tells us that he was on Patmos "because of the word of God" (1:9), so it is equally likely he was there undertaking missionary activity, much like other apostles such as Paul or Barnabas.

What Sort of Writing Is It?

Revelation, as a type of literature, can feel mixed and chaotic to read. I personally think this is intentional. An unusual amount of sentences in Revelation start with "and" (Greek: *kai*), conveying a sense of urgency to readers.[5] From the opening vision alone (1:12–20) we get the following:

---

[5] *Kai* is sometimes translated "then" or "but" or "even" in English Bibles. It can have all these senses depending on context. Sometimes, the English translators have changed it up to make the English a bit more readable.

- *And* I turned to see the voice… (1:12)
- *And* turning I saw… (1:12)
- *And* in the middle of the lampstands… (1:13)
- *And* his feet … *and* his voice… (1:15)
- *And* having in his right hand… (1:16)
- *And* when I saw him… (1:17)
- *And* he placed his hand on me… (1:17)

And I saw…and then…and I saw…and I saw…and then…and… and… John cleverly draws us into his experience, encouraging us to look around with him as he tries to take in everything he sees. It feels frantic and urgent because the author wants us to know it is. It is also highly visual. Things are revealed to John primarily through the sense of sight. He sees stuff! God's angel takes him on a visual tour of the earth and heavens. This makes Revelation different from most prophetic literature of the Bible, where God's word is disclosed through hearing God speak in some way.

Apocalypse as a Genre

As a genre or style of writing, Revelation has been viewed as typical of an ancient apocalypse. This kind of literature takes different forms and has its beginnings in Second Temple Judaism (516 BCE–70 CE), possibly influenced by Persian religion.[6]

The definition of apocalypse commonly used in biblical studies today emerged from conversations between scholars in the 1970s:

> An apocalypse is a genre of revelatory literature within a narrative framework, in which a revelation is mediated by an otherworldly being to a human recipient, disclosing a transcendent reality which

---

[6] The Jews lived under Persian rule from 539–332 BCE, so they could not have avoided some contact with Zoroastrianism. Zoroastrianism is a Persian (Iranian) religion known for its dualistic tendencies and its emphasis on the battle between good and evil.

is both temporal, insofar as it envisages eschatological salvation, and spatial insofar as it involves another, supernatural world.[7]

Let's break this down. Apocalypses are narratives where something is disclosed from a supernatural source. In the case of Revelation, John tells us he receives instructions and visions from God, but these are mediated through angels. These visions have two dimensions—spatial and temporal. The spatial dimension in Revelation is that John goes up to heaven and sees God and the heavenly courtroom. He moves around the cosmos to view God's realm and also to view the earth from God's perspective. In doing so, John reveals to readers what they cannot see from their own location. He reveals something spatial. The temporal dimension is that John also seems to move through time, seeing things that have not yet happened but will happen soon. He is given a glimpse of the future. John is both a time traveler and a space traveler in Revelation.

In many ways, this definition of apocalypse is helpful for pointing out the main dynamics of a text like Revelation, but it doesn't really tell us the purpose. The why. What function does John's apocalypse serve? Other scholars have pointed out this lack and have suggested that we also need to note that John's time-space travel revelation is intended to influence the behavior of the audience, to persuade them of something. I suggest that this "something" is threefold: worship, witness, and wait. We'll return to these more fully later.

Apocalyptic literature has several features that make it different to a lot of the other writing in the Bible. It is:

- highly visual: information is disclosed primarily through visions, dreams, and journeys to other realms;
- intensely symbolic: it draws on myths and cultural traditions, often layered and numerous;

---

[7]John Collins, "Introduction: Towards the Morphology of a Genre," *Semeia* 14 (1979): 1–14 (quotation from p.1).

- dualistic: the world is divided into evil/good, present/future, wicked/righteous, earth/heaven;
- supernatural: angels and other heavenly beings act as guides;
- pseudonymous: authorship is attributed to someone from the past, like Enoch, Ezra, or Daniel (Revelation might be the exception to this general trend);
- catastrophic: it imagines some kind of judgment or cosmic event that changes everything.

To complicate matters, Revelation describes itself as both an apocalypse (1:1) and a prophecy (1:3; 19:10; 22:7, 10, 18–19). This pairing makes sense, since apocalyptic thinking emerged out of prophetic traditions. It also contains sections that look a lot like letters (chapters 2–3). Given we find a number of different genres within Revelation, it might be more important to look at what it contains and what it *does*, rather than trying to fit it into a genre definition.

An Apocalyptic Worldview

Behind apocalyptic literature as a type of writing lies a worldview that we also describe as "apocalyptic." This is a much broader category than just a type of writing. The rise of apocalyptic thinking in the two hundred or so years before Jesus is not fully understood, but we know that during this time, theological attitudes and ways of viewing the world shifted within Judaism.

Some of the more important shifts include the idea of a righteous sufferer (martyr) and belief in a future resurrection of the dead. These ideas are obviously linked, but let's deal with suffering first. In classical biblical prophecy, the suffering of the nation was interpreted by prophets as punishment for the people's sin. Communal sins included things like idolatry, injustice, or generally disobeying God's law. When the nation of Israel suffered, the prophets held up a mirror and asked them to examine themselves, repent, and turn back to God.

This kind of theology stops making sense when a righteous person suffers. When good and faithful people are suffering, there has to be a theological way to account for how justice will be done. In the book of Daniel, Daniel and his friends face suffering not because they have disobeyed God's law but because they are faithful Jews living in a hostile culture. The book explores and responds to this experience, offering a way to understand what might be happening when righteous people suffer. Instead of locating the sin, or evil, within the person or community, it was conceptualized as an external force, placing pressure on the community from the outside. Evil was something that acted against God's faithful people. We see this idea emerge more fully in the Maccabean literature, which depicts faithful Jews being forced to make sacrifices to foreign gods or eat pork meat: when they refused, they were put to death (1 Maccabees 2:15–38, 2 Maccabees 6:7–7:42).[8] And so the idea of the righteous martyr was born. Faithful Jews suffered because they were faithful, not because they were unfaithful.

Hope of future resurrection, future rewards and punishments, and divine intervention were ways of saying that God would address present earthly injustice. While there are many images of restoration in the Hebrew Bible, the idea of resurrection from the dead to eternal life is explicitly stated for the first time in Daniel 12:2, one of the latest compositions in the Hebrew Bible. The author writes that "those who sleep in the dust of the earth [a metaphor for death] shall awake, some to everlasting life and some to shame and everlasting contempt." These beliefs in eternal reward or punishment grew from a refusal to acknowledge that the present world was the ultimate reality and that earthly injustice would not be rectified by God.

If this all sounds rather strange to you, then consider this: the entire New Testament is deeply apocalyptic. Jesus's death and resurrection make no sense without an apocalyptic view of the world. Jesus died

---

[8] The Torah forbids Jews from eating pork as it was considered an unclean animal (Leviticus 11:7). It therefore became a way for those outside the Jewish community to test or torture Jews.

as a type of righteous martyr, an utterly faithful Jew who was killed by the powers of evil and sin. His resurrection, in the New Testament, is framed as his vindication, and evidence that God will deal with the forces of sin and death by overturning them. This is classic apocalyptic thinking, and in this regard, Revelation is much like a version of the rest of the New Testament, but on steroids.

Apocalyptic Theology

We have already noted the apocalyptic nature of John's theology, which makes it dualistic and combative. John is also steeped in the Hebrew Bible and assumes his audience knows these stories, too. We shall see that elements of Isaiah, Ezekiel, and Daniel appear frequently in the book of Revelation, as do grand themes like the plagues of Egypt that are part of the exodus story (Exodus 7–12). In drawing on these Hebrew Bible traditions, John wanted his readers to know that the same God who freed the Hebrews from enslavement in Egypt had freed them from the powers of evil and oppression in their own day.

John assumes his audience knows the basic Jesus story as told in the Gospels. He doesn't take time to narrate information about Jesus's life, death, or resurrection, but refers to these with a variety of symbols that indicate his interest is in the significance of the Christ event. Jesus appears in several guises in Revelation, each with its own theological nuance. In one scene, he is like a Son of Man shining in his statuesque splendor (1:12–20); in another, he is a lion-like multi-headed Lamb who has been slaughtered but is alive (5:5–6); in yet another, he is a cavalry commander riding to war on his white horse (19:11–16). Jesus is all these things, as well as martyr (1:5), morning star (22:16), bridegroom (19:7), and king of kings (17:14; 19:16). These images hold together the vulnerable and intimate human Jesus with the all-powerful warrior Jesus who is capable of conquering evil.

As we view Revelation from 30,000 feet, we also need to pay attention to the importance of power in this text. In many ways, we can read this book as a narration of a grand cosmic power battle—a battle the author wants you to know God has already won. The first few verses of Revelation are thick with language pertaining to power: dominion, all-mighty, ruler, power, kingdom, to mention just a few (1:4–8). God's power is total: only here in the New Testament is God described as all-mighty or all-powerful (Greek: *panto-krator*, 1:8). Jesus, too, is described as a ruler who will rule with a "rod of iron" (12:5; 19:15) over the kings of the earth (1:5), and he is later hailed as "king of kings and lord of lords" (19:16).

God's power is described as something that lasts "forever and ever" (1:6). Alpha and omega, the first and last letters of the Greek alphabet, are one way the author conveys the timelessness of God, who is both the beginning and the goal of all things. Similarly, God's title as one "who was, who is, and who is coming" also points to his eternal nature. This aspect of God's power will be juxtaposed with the temporal and temporary power of Rome and Rome's emperor.

In the midst of the multiple assertions of divine power come words of comfort and tenderness. This all-mighty God loves and frees humans and wants them to be part of the kingdom (1:6–7). Ultimately, God comes towards humanity in Revelation, moving from the heavenly throne room to live with people from all nations on earth in the New Jerusalem (21:3–22). This is no escapist text. It is a radical affirmation that the creator and ruler of the cosmos so desperately wants to live with creation that God will make a home among mortals.

But we are jumping ahead! Let us first take a look at what messages John has from Jesus for the Christian communities living in Asia Minor in the first century CE.

CHAPTER TWO

Messages to the Seven Communities

The book of Revelation starts out a bit like an ancient letter. It has a greeting, a doxology,[1] an author, and named recipients, although not in the order we usually get them in other ancient epistles. The first two verses function almost as a title announcing what to expect—a "revelation" of Jesus from God. Then John offers words of blessing for all those who read aloud and hear the words that follow. The blessing reminds us contemporary readers of how ancient Christian communities encountered what we now call the Bible.[2] They *heard* it read aloud. The blessing, however, does not come only from hearing the words of prophecy but also from *keeping* them (1:3). John imparts a tone of urgency with the words "for the time is near," as he wants his words to have an actual impact on human behavior.

After the blessing, John greets the specific communities he will address in more detail in Revelation 2 and 3, offering them "grace and

---

[1] A doxology is a praise hymn. E.g. "to him be glory and power for ever and ever, Amen" (Revelation 1:6).
[2] I am using "Christian" for simplicity, but we should note that this term was not used to denote a distinct group until the late first or early second century, where it was first used by outsiders (see Acts 11:26). The earliest followers of Jesus were Jews, and John seems to be writing to predominantly Jewish Christ-believers.

peace" (1:4). The recipients are the seven churches in Asia Minor. You can still visit archaeological sites in most of these Turkish towns today; you will not, however, find a Christian church among the ruins, at least not one from the first century. So even though your Bible might use the language of "church" in Revelation 1–3, we are talking about communities of believers, not buildings. The Greek word translated "church" is *ekklesia*, and it means an assembly or gathering of people. In the first century CE, it denoted a wide variety of community, religious, and political organizations. Seven is the number of perfection, so when John addresses the "seven churches," he is addressing both specific communities and the universal or whole church. His messages might go to seven specific communities in Asia Minor, but they have implications for believers far beyond those communities.

John greets this universal community of believers using a threefold description of God. This is not the Trinity in the sense that is later developed in Christian creeds,[3] but it does reflect a basic pattern of Creator God, Jesus, and Spirit. However, because nothing is straightforward in Revelation, different language and imagery are used for each aspect of the divine.

The title John uses for God is "the one who is, who was, and who is coming" (1:4, 8). This emphasizes the eternal nature of God as one who has always been, is present now, and will be more fully present on earth at some point in the future. The image he uses a few verses later of "alpha and omega" (the first and last letters of the Greek alphabet) communicates the same thing (1:8). God is the A and Z, the beginning and the end of all things. The Spirit is closely associated with God and described as the "seven spirits," symbolizing the universal or perfect Spirit of God. These seven spirits will roam the earth acting as God's eyes and ears, namely, God's presence on earth (5:6).

---

[3] The term "Trinity" is not found in the Bible although God is described in a variety of ways including, but not limited to, Father, Son, and Spirit. The doctrine of the Trinity was developed in the centuries following the New Testament and formalized for the first time at the Council of Nicaea in 325 CE using the traditional language of Father, Son, and Holy Spirit.

Jesus is described in these opening verses of Revelation 1:1–8 in a way that summarizes his death, resurrection, and ascension, but not in obvious or typical language. Nowhere does John retell the basic Jesus story: he simply assumes his audience knows it. But he does refer to the key events of the crucifixion, resurrection, and ascension in a variety of ways. Here, he uses images of martyrdom, rebirth, and kingship. Jesus is the "faithful witness [Greek: *martyr*]," the "firstborn of the dead," and "ruler of the kings of the earth" (1:5). Witnessing is one of the most important things a follower of Jesus can do in Revelation, partly because, in this way, they imitate Christ. But witnessing in Revelation is about more than making speeches or sharing personal testimonies about Jesus, although it might include those aspects. Witnessing has already taken on some of the later resonances of martyrdom. After all, the English word martyr comes from the Greek words for witness— *martyr, martyria*. While *martyr* in Greek can simply mean someone who testifies or witnesses to something, witnesses in Revelation are those who have died for their testimony, like Jesus (1:5), Antipas (2:13), and the saints under the altar who were slaughtered because of their witness (6:9). As martyr and firstborn, Jesus was dead but is now raised. The last part is just as important: Jesus now rules over all earthly rulers. This is a political claim as much as it is a religious one, and it has implications for Christians in the Roman Empire in terms of their relationship with authorities like the Roman emperor and his agents.

Finally, John ends this introduction in Revelation 1 with a doxology that is a summary of both his theology and his understanding of the gospel. This is typical of ancient Christian letters, where a doxology is added to the opening greetings (see, for example, 1 Corinthians 1:3; Philemon 1:3; 1 Peter 1:2–3).

If we follow John's understanding of the significance of Jesus, it goes something like this:

- Jesus loves us.
- Jesus's death and resurrection has released us from sin.

- Jesus has made us a priestly kingdom to serve the all-powerful God.

This Jesus, described as coming with the clouds (1:7), is the one whom readers encounter in the very next scene through John's description of his vision of "one like a son of man."

The Opening Vision (1:9–20)

"Write What You See"

The opening vision that begins in 1:9 serves as a commissioning narrative as well as an epiphany. After telling us that he is on Patmos, John presents himself as a prophetic figure who is "in the spirit" and hears a voice speaking with him. This voice, which sounds like a trumpet, tells him to "write in a book what you see and send it to the seven churches" (1:11). This time, the seven churches are named (more on those later).

Seeing is central in Revelation. We shall discover that eyes are everywhere, and many of the heavenly creatures have supernatural sight like God. But sight goes in both directions. Readers will encounter a God who sees humanity; but just as remarkable, it is primarily through sight that John receives knowledge of both God and what God is doing. It is as if he is watching a private movie and describing it to us in detail. This differs from the usual pattern of biblical prophecy, where God's wisdom is primarily communicated through words. Think, for example, of the numerous occasions where the Bible describes that "the word of the LORD came to _____" (e.g., Genesis 15:1, Jeremiah 1:4) or where it describes God speaking as a formless voice (e.g., Deuteronomy 4:12).

The command to "write what you see" is repeated at the end of the opening vision (1:19), with the clarification that John sees things that are now and also will be. That is, he is seeing things about the current world that reveal it for how it truly is, *and* he is seeing things that look to the future and unveil something of God's plans. We should not think of this future aspect as a kind of predictive prophecy but rather more like the visions of hope we find in other parts of the Bible, which use metaphors of bones regrowing into living beings (Ezekiel 37), nations streaming to Mount Zion (Isaiah 18; Micah 4), feasting, weddings, and other joyful scenes of abundance as a way to communicate hope for a better future.

The verbal commission in Revelation 1:19 immediately gives way to the visual in a reversal of the usual direction of biblical prophetic encounters with God. The contents of what John is to write will not be what he hears, but what he sees.

Who Is the "One Like a Son of Man"?

John describes hearing a voice that sounds like a trumpet. Yet, when he turns to see the sound, he does not see a trumpeter but instead observes seven golden lampstands with a figure standing in their midst (1:12–13). Who is this figure and what is the significance of the images used to describe him?

The figure is "like a son of man." "Son of Man" language comes from the prophetic tradition in the Hebrew Bible, where it often means something like "human." For example, Ezekiel is addressed as "son of man," usually translated "mortal" (Ezekiel 2:1). Daniel sees a vision of one "like a son of a human" coming with the clouds (Daniel 7:13), a verse alluded to in Revelation 1:7. Both instances use a combination of the Aramaic or Hebrew word for son and the word for human to denote a human-like figure (see also Psalm 8:4; 80:17). By the time the New Testament is written, Son of Man has become a messianic title, and we see it used in this way in all four of the Gospels. The grammar nerds among you might like to note that in the Gospels it takes the definite article: Jesus is "*the* son of a human"—indicating its function as a title—not an indefinite "*a* son of a human."

Much has been written about what this Son of Man language means and how it functions in the Gospels. It is apocalyptic language that carries with it a set of messianic expectations. Messiah (Greek: *christos* or Christ) simply means "anointed one". There was a great deal of diversity regarding the Messiah in first century Judaism—he might be a healer, prophet, king, or liberator—and several Jewish leaders were given the title Messiah in the first century CE. Son of Man is therefore only one concept, amongst many, when it comes to Jewish ideas about the Messiah. It is, however, the one we find mostly in Jewish apocalyptic texts and is associated with the idea of someone who will come to judge the wicked and redeem God's people. What we do know is that Jesus referred to himself this way and others used it to describe Jesus. When they did, they were saying something about Jesus's status as the anticipated Messiah of Israel, whose appearance represents God breaking into the world.

As hearer-readers of these visions, we encounter things in the order John recounts them; we only see what he sees and in the order he narrates it. We first get a general impression of a human-like figure in a long robe with a golden sash. These images are drawn from Daniel 10:5, where an angelic figure is described in very similar ways. Indeed, many of the images used in Revelation 1:12–20 are from Daniel 10, adding a layer of ambiguity to the imagery: this one like a Son of Man is clearly Christ-like in aspects but also very close to Daniel's angel.

As he describes the figure standing among the lampstands, John starts from the figure's head and moves down. Ancient rhetorical literature advises that this was the best way to describe a person when giving a vivid depiction of them.[4] The figure's hair is white like white wool, his eyes like flames of fire. Notice these qualifiers throughout: "like"

---

[4] Aphthonius, *Progymnasmata*, 12. Aphthonius was a Greek rhetorician from Antioch who lived in the fourth century CE. He wrote about how to vividly describe someone in his Early Exercises (Greek: progymnasmata) for school students.

and "as." It is as if the figure is indescribable, therefore John can only recount his features by analogy.

While many of these images are familiar from Daniel, Ezekiel, and other ancient Jewish texts (such as 1 Maccabees and 1 Enoch),[5] the sheer density of them is staggering. John has layered symbols from various figures in the tradition to create a bright, shining, dangerous, royal, priestly, and divine figure.

The location of the Son of Man figure is very important: he stands in the middle of the seven lampstands. These lampstands are the first thing John sees, and they are one of only two features (the other being the seven stars) that the angelic messenger explicitly interprets so that John and the recipients of the vision cannot miss their significance. These seven lampstands are symbols for the seven churches (1:20), which means that the terrifying and strange Son of Man figure is standing right in the midst of these churches. He is there, close by! And he has something to say to them.

The Effect of the Vision and Commission

When John sees the Son of Man standing among the lampstands, he falls down as though dead (1:17). It seems rather dramatic! In the biblical tradition, however, seeing God can be dangerous. Indeed, in Revelation 6:16, God's face is associated with divine wrath, and the people cry out, wanting to hide from the face of God. John's reaction tells us he recognizes he has just seen the divine, and he passes out at the thought, perhaps overwhelmed by his own fear. Jesus reassures him, saying "do not be afraid," and restores him with a touch.

---

[5] 1 Enoch is a Jewish apocalyptic text that dates from approximately 300 to 100 BCE. It is cited in Jude and was clearly known to the authors of the New Testament, including John. Enoch is the name of one of Jared's sons who was "taken" by God (Genesis 5:21–24) leading to speculation that he, like Elijah, was taken up and didn't die.

Being told not to be afraid is a bit like being told not to be anxious—pretty unhelpful. In fact, it mostly affirms one's anxiety or fear. This is precisely how John's rhetoric is working here. By modelling fear in the face of the divine, John is embodying the appropriate response to Jesus's presence—fear.

According to the ancient philosopher Aristotle, fear is a great motivator, but it only works as a motivator if the thing we fear is nearby or immediate.[6] For example, if someone tells us our house will burn down in twenty years, we probably wouldn't change anything about our behavior right now. We can worry about it later. But if someone warns us that our house will burn down tonight, we might check the electrics and fire-alarms and make sure there aren't any open flames. In Revelation, the appeal to fear works because Christ is among the lampstands, and the lampstands are the churches. Jesus is right in their midst in all his terrifying glory. Be alert!

We learn one more thing about Jesus in this opening vision. As he assures John not to be afraid, he affirms his identity as the one who was dead, is risen, and now lives forever (1:17–18). Jesus's risen status is given as the reason he now has the key to unlock the power of Death and Hades (the realm of the dead). To find out what that means and what he is going to do with this key, we have to keep reading.

The Messages (Revelation 2–3)

Chapters 2–3 of Revelation contain seven messages to seven Christian communities in Asia Minor. These messages follow a formulaic pattern:

- a command to write: "To the angel of the church in XX, write…"
- a description of Christ who is speaking
- a description of the local situation: "I know…"
- an accusation or area for improvement

---

[6] Aristotle, *Rhetoric*, book 2.

- an exhortation to repent or remain faithful
- a call: "let anyone who has an ear listen…"
- a promise or reward for the faithful

These seven messages are presented as if they are the direct words of the risen Christ, who was revealed in the preceding vision (1:12–20). Each one is introduced with the phrase, "these are the words," which is a version of the prophetic formula "thus says the LORD." Christ is variously described as the one who walks among the lampstands holding the seven stars; the one who was dead but is alive; the one with the sharp two-edged sword; the one with eyes of flaming fire and feet of burnished bronze; the one who has the seven spirits of God; the one who has the key; and the one who is the faithful witness. In many cases, the image used to describe Christ relates to the contents of the particular message. For example, the church in Pergamum is addressed by the figure of Jesus described as the one "who has the sharp two-edged sword"—a menacing symbol—and is threatened with war from that sword if the people do not repent of certain teachings.

Conveyed as the words of the risen Christ, these messages are some of the few passages in Revelation where we hear rather than see what God communicates. Jesus speaks, and what he says relates to the particular struggles of each community. Yet, despite the particularity, we also find common themes across these messages: encouragement to remain faithful in the face of hostility, a reminder not to become complacent, and, in the strongest messages, a call to repent of wrong teaching and idolatrous behavior.

Encouragement: Hold Fast!

The mildest messages are those to Smyrna and Philadelphia, which primarily contain encouragement. Jesus acknowledges that the community in Smyrna is poor, but he affirms them as spiritually rich. Members of the community in Philadelphia are affirmed for their good works despite having little power. Alongside the recognition that both of these communities might be poor or powerless in worldly terms, there is also the acknowledgment of danger. Both face hostility and are exhorted to remain faithful in the face of impending suffering.

Ancient Smyrna was a large port city featuring a theatre, temples, a stadium, gymnasium, baths, and a library typical of a sizable Greco-Roman city. There was significant wealth in the city, and there was also an established Jewish community (see 1 Maccabees 15). Philadelphia was an inland city in a fertile area where vines and other crops grew. It had a mixed population and was home to temples dedicated to various gods as well as a cult for the emperor Augustus. According to ancient sources, there was also a Jewish community in Philadelphia.

It is likely that the hostility faced by both these communities came from tension with the local Jewish community rather than with the empire, even though Smyrna contained a provincial temple to the emperor (see more on these temples below). There are strong words about "those who say they are Jews but are not" and those who are "a synagogue of Satan" (2:9; 3:9). We should recognize this as highly contextual rhetorical language. The second century CE *Martyrdom of Polycarp*, which is also set in Smyrna, similarly blames Jews for inciting violence against Christians, perhaps repeating the kind of polemic we get here between these two closely related religious communities.

Historically, it is quite likely that Jewish communities were distancing themselves from Christians and perhaps even expelling them from the synagogue on the basis that their beliefs were blasphemous. The Philadelphians are praised by Jesus for "not denying my name" (3:8), indicating that confessions about Jesus may be central to the conflict, and there may have been pressure to deny Jesus as Messiah. That Christ is described as the one holding the key of David (3:7) is a way of signaling that Jesus is the Messiah expected from the Davidic line. This key of David opens a door that cannot be shut. Here, we can see a play on the idea that Jesus-followers might have been shut out of the synagogue, but Jesus has opened a different door.

We should note that such tensions were localized, not universal, and there is evidence that, in many places, Jews and Christians shared synagogues for centuries. Where Jews were expelled from their communities for following Christ, they would not only have been separated from family members but also removed from the protection (marginal though it may be) of association with Judaism and the wealth and networks of these communities.

The Christians in Smyrna and Philadelphia are exhorted to "hold fast" and "be faithful," even in the face of death. If they do so, they will receive eternal life. This is symbolized in the promises of a crown of life (2:10), protection from the second death (2:11), and the bestowal of a new name in the city of God (3:12).

Complacency: Wake Up!

Three of the messages in Revelation 2–3 seem more concerned with complacency than anything else. Ephesus, Sardis, and Laodicea are all affirmed for some things and rebuked for others. Their messages contain a combination of calls to repentance and encouragement to wake up, listen, and pay attention to what God is doing.

The first of these messages is to the Christian community in Ephesus. Ancient Ephesus was a distinguished city—a large, port town that was cosmopolitan and famous for its temple to the goddess Artemis, its library dating to the second century CE, and its theatre. A temple to "the Sebastoi" (venerable ones) was built by Emperor Domitian around 89–90 CE and dedicated to the imperial family. This shows the reach of the Roman Empire, whose presence was felt and represented in these provincial or imperial temples that dominated the landscape.

The Christians in Ephesus are commended for their works and endurance, and for having tested false teachers. But they are accused of abandoning their first love (2:4). What this specifically means is unclear, but it likely points to a loss of the conviction and passion that followed their conversion. Jesus's threat to them is that they will lose their identity as a Christian community, symbolized by the removal of their lampstand. Their reward for being faithful is to eat from the tree of life in the eternal city of God.

Members of the community in Sardis are accused of a kind of ambivalence toward their faith. Their works are not perfect, and they look like they are alive but they "are dead" (3:1–2). Some in the community are worthy, but others need to "wake up," strengthen their faith, and obey the teaching they first heard. Those who "conquer" by staying faithful will receive a white robe and have their names remain in the book of life, both of which are further symbols of eternal life.

The last community to fall into this group are the Christians in Laodicea. Lying inland from Ephesus, ancient Laodicea was a wealthy city that also sat on a trade route. Like other significant cities in Asia Minor, it had baths, a gymnasium, two theatres, temples, and a huge stadium thought to seat about 25,000 people, who would come to watch athletic events, gladiator fights, and public executions. The city also had a significant Jewish community.

Laodicea was famous for a couple of things. First, it was known for its medical expertise, based on a long and gruesome history of experimenting on prisoners. Its medical school was a leader in anatomy and ophthalmology. The Greek historian and geographer Strabo mentions its famous eye salve. The same word for salve (Greek: *kollourion*) is used in Revelation 3:18, where Jesus advises the Laodicean community to "anoint your eyes" with salve so they can see properly. It is a clever play on the local culture by John, who portrays Jesus using local medical knowledge to remind the community they do not see things clearly in spiritual terms.

Second, Laodicea had an elaborate water distribution system, which drew water from the nearby rivers and hot springs. The water that came from Pamukkale (Hierapolis) was sourced from mineral hot springs, which you can still visit and bathe in today. Coming several miles via aqueduct, the water that was hot in Pamukkale was lukewarm by the time it arrived in Laodicea. The statement that the community members are "neither hot nor cold" but lukewarm draws on this local knowledge to accuse them of being dispassionate about their faith (3:15–16). Lukewarm water is not particularly nice to drink, something our author alludes to with the statement that Jesus will spit them out of his mouth! In John's theology, you are either a hundred percent Team Jesus or you are nothing. This community appears to be the opposite of Ephesus and Sardis. They are accused of thinking they are rich (which they may have been in worldly terms) when they are actually poor, pitiable, and naked when it comes to faith. Their sin is having a false sense of their situation. Yet, if they repent and listen to Jesus, they are promised a share of his throne and thus his eternal reign.

Idolatry: Repent!

The last two messages to discuss here are those to Pergamum and Thyatira. These contain the strongest condemnation along with a clear call to repentance and a threat of what will happen if they do not repent. These two communities are accused of eating idol meat and practicing fornication, of tolerating someone called Jezebel, and of supporting the teaching of the Nicolaitans. John also references a strange story involving Balak and Balaam. There is a lot to unpack here, so we will take a bit more time. Let's begin with what we know about these communities.

Thyatira is mentioned elsewhere in the New Testament, in Acts 16:11–40, where it is the home of Lydia, a convert of Paul. Like many of the other cities mentioned in Revelation, the Christian community there is connected with Paul's missionary activity. We have less archaeological evidence for ancient Thyatira than we do for some of the other cities, but what exists suggests it had a lively trade culture of wool, linen, pottery, metalworking, and dye. It too had a variety of temples and cults to different gods and emperors, like Athena, Zeus, Apollo, and Demeter. Interestingly, Demeter was usually depicted holding a fiery torch. Perhaps the description of Christ as the one with eyes like flames of fire and feet like burnished bronze (2:18) is a deliberate nod to these local cult and trade practices.

Pergamum was a famous town in antiquity and one we know much more about. It sat on an important trade route and boasted a library, a theatre, and a medical center later associated with the famous medic

Galen. It also held one of the first provincial temples, which was built around 29 BCE and dedicated to the goddess Roma and the emperor Augustus (Octavian). This temple became known as a location for the imperial cult, which is exactly what it sounds like. Imperial cults were cults set up in honor of the emperor. While it can be challenging to accurately reconstruct ancient worship practices on the basis of inscriptions, coins, archaeology, and historical accounts, we have good evidence to suggest their practices included a range of religious-type activities we might associate with temples or churches today. These activities included an official priestly order, a sacrificial system where food and drink offerings were made to the emperor and his family (along with certain gods), hymns of praise that were sung to the emperor, statues and other visual iconography that were produced and dedicated, and key dates celebrated with festivals.[7]

Pergamum was also the location of a famous altar to Zeus, built into an acropolis on the hill in the second century BCE. Zeus was the highest of the Greek gods, and this altar is so grand that an entire museum in Berlin is dedicated to it. In the museum, the altar has been rebuilt (with both original and reconstructed parts) in full size, which is around forty feet high. The friezes around the altar are covered with elaborate carvings of mythical battles between the gods, humans, and giants. Some scholars think that the "throne of Satan" mentioned in 2:13 is a reference to this altar. Pergamum also had temples for the emperor Trajan and goddess Athena, but one did not have to visit Pergamum to know about its temples and altars. The Romans produced coins with images that showed the provincial temple and emperor. These were widely dispersed, spreading imperial propaganda throughout Asia Minor.

Christians in Pergamum seem to have been under some physical threat, and someone named Antipas had died for his witness to Jesus

---

[7] For more details about the history and archaeology, see Steven J. Friesen, *Imperial Cults and the Apocalypse of John: Reading Revelation in the Ruins* (Oxford: Oxford University Press, 2001)

(2:13). They are commended for their faith in the face of such hostility. However, the risen Christ takes issue with some of their teaching and calls them to repent. It seems they have been eating the meat from local cults—that is, meat that had been sacrificed to Zeus, other gods, or the emperor. For John, this is akin to participating in the actual worship of these foreign gods and leaders. It is idolatry. This is where Balaam and Jezebel come in.

Balaam and Jezebel are not the names of actual people, but rather famous Gentiles from the Hebrew Bible. Both led the people of God astray in convincing them to worship other deities. Balaam was a prophet who was commanded by the Moabite king Balak to curse Israel. To his credit, he blessed them instead. Despite this, he is remembered in the Hebrew Bible as a foreigner who led the Israelites to worship Baal and therefore commit idolatry (see Numbers 22–25). In the Numbers account, Balaam is eventually killed by the Israelites with a sword (Numbers 31:8). Notably, in the introduction to the message to Pergamum, Jesus is described as the one with a sharp, two-edged sword as a clever way of connecting the two situations.

Jezebel is almost certainly a rude nickname given to a real female prophet who is a rival teacher to John. In calling her "Jezebel," John is using a moniker that implies she is an idol-worshiping foreigner who leads everyone astray. In the story from 1 Kings, Jezebel is the foreign wife of King Ahab (1 Kings 16). She worships Baal and convinces her husband to do unethical things, like steal Naboth's vineyard and kill the prophets of God. For her crimes, she is ultimately killed, and her body is eaten by dogs in a gruesome and violent scene (2 Kings 9). It is interesting that John never criticizes the woman he calls Jezebel for being a woman *per se*; that is, this is not about a woman's teaching role within the congregation. John does, however, have massive issues with the content of her teaching.

Jezebel seems to have been teaching the community in Thyatira that it is alright for Christ-followers to buy and eat the meat sacrificed to other gods in the marketplace. The reality is that most meat at the time was sacrificial meat, so it would have been hard to find meat that had not been first offered to a god or the emperor. Whether or not Christians should eat such meat seems to have been a contentious topic in early Christianity. Paul addresses the question in his letter to the Corinthians, advising that such meat is empty of power because these other gods have no real power (see 1 Corinthians 8:1–13). He acknowledges that this can be a stumbling block for some, so caution is needed. On the other hand, the author of Luke-Acts advises believers to abstain from eating such meat, associating it with fornication (Acts 15:29; 21:25). John is even stronger in his approach to the matter. For him, partaking of meat associated with other religious practices is a type of idolatry that he calls *porneuo* (a Greek word that means "sexual immorality" or "fornication" or "prostitution").[8]

When John writes that the community in Thyatira "eat food sacrificed to idols and practice fornication [Greek: *porneuo*]" (2:14; 2:20), he is not referring to two different things; rather, he is making the point that idolatry *is* sexual immorality. The technical grammatical term for this is an ep-exegetical *kai* (an explanatory *kai*). As I mentioned earlier, *kai* is a Greek word that can mean "and," "that," "even," and sometimes "but." It is flexible. When it occurs in this kind of construction, it acts as a joining word indicating the thing that follows is an explanation of the first thing. So, if you are still reading after that bit of technical grammar, we might better translate this verse, "they eat food sacrificed to idols, *that is,* practice fornication" (2:14). Or, in the reverse direction as in 2:20, they "practice fornication, *that is,* eat idol meat." Here, John is drawing on Jewish understandings of God's covenantal relationship with God's people. In the biblical tradition, when God's people worship other gods, they are committing a kind of adultery—they are cheating on God (see Hosea for a good example of this kind of prophetic thinking). John does not have sexual activity in mind here. He is concerned with worship and fidelity to God, because worshiping God alone is one of his big concerns. The way he conveys

---

[8] The porn- part of this word has been retained in the contemporary English word "pornography."

this is to point out that if you are worshiping other gods or kings, including eating meat sacrificed to them, you are cheating on God. You are religiously promiscuous.

Which brings us to the Nicolaitans. Who are they? In short, we don't know. These two verses (2:6, 15) are the only references to them in ancient Christian or Jewish literature, so we have to look at the context to make sense of the reference. Ephesus is congratulated for hating the Nicolatians' works which, according to Jesus, "I also hate" (2:6). Clearly, they are on the bad list. Pergamum is rebuked because some of its members hold to the Nicolaitans' teaching (2:15). This rebuke follows directly after the critique of Balaam's teaching about eating idol meat. In its context following the rebuke, it appears the Nicolaitans are another group who teach that participating in the local cults is permitted for Christians. John clearly disagrees!

Why All these Messages?

We have seen that John draws on local knowledge to personalize and give color to the seven messages to the seven churches. It is a reminder that real places and communities are being addressed and their context is important. These messages, however, also function at a broader level. The number seven is the number of perfection or universality; there is therefore a sense that, in addressing these seven communities, John is addressing the whole Christian community. The general themes of exhortation to repent of false teaching, idolatry, or complacency and the call to hold fast and remember one's first love in faith could be applied to almost any situation or Christian group. At stake, at least for John, is one's place in the eternal city of God.

CHAPTER THREE

Game of Thrones

At the beginning of Revelation 4, a door stands open. It's not a normal door. This is the door to the heavenly realm, and it is a sign that
any perceived barrier between heaven and earth is about to be broken down. John is invited by the Son of Man figure from the opening
vision to "come up here," and he finds himself transported into the
heavenly throne room. The reason he is there is so that God can show
him "what must take place" (4:1). Now we get to the heart of Revelation and the start of the main vision that dominates the book.

As modern readers, we are inevitably tempted to ask whether this
actually happened. But if we return to our commitment to read Revelation through ancient eyes, the question of whether this happened—or
whether it might be explained in another way, such as through a dream
or an ecstatic experience—is neither a question we can answer, nor one
an ancient audience might have asked. For audiences steeped in the
biblical tradition, being "in the spirit" is a way of describing prophetic
activity, and being transported to another realm is quite typical in
apocalyptic texts. It signals to readers that what follows comes directly
from the divine realm and is given to the prophet from God. What
John is doing here is making a claim about truthfulness and authority.

Throughout this vision (Revelation 4 onwards is one long vision),
John uses symbols in slightly unusual ways. Sometimes he stacks them
up densely, and the effect can be dazzling. At other times, he uses symbols that stand in tension—or even contradict one another—to create

something new. For example, the Jesus we meet in Revelation 5 is both a lion and a lamb, both slain and resurrected. His wounds suggest vulnerability, yet his seven horns suggest complete power. This is the kind of cognitive dissonance that we have to grapple with in Revelation.

Our task as we get into the details of the vision is not to map out every single symbol and find its precise precedent or possible referents. (Scholars have done this to death, and it gets pretty boring). Nor can I tell you that X definitely means Y. That kind of attempt to decode Revelation leads to all sorts of problematic interpretations, such as trying to predict the date of Jesus's return based on the Euphrates drying up. (Read Revelation 16:12, then search "Euphrates and Revelation" online…or don't.) Our task, rather, is to let the images wash over us as we read and to be aware of their effect. We might ask ourselves the following questions as we read these passages in Revelation: What is new in John's descriptions? What is familiar? What is it about this scene that challenges our understanding of God? What does it affirm? What does John want us to feel? And what does John want us to know?

The Heavenly Throne Room (4:1–11)

After going through the open door, John finds himself in heaven, where he first notices a throne and then sees the one seated upon it (4:2). This is one of the most common ways John will describe God throughout Revelation—as one seated upon a throne—and this points to God's rule and power being essential elements of John's theology. For John, the only thing worse than God not doing something to look after Christians on earth is God being impotent or incapable of caring for, vindicating, and protecting them.

If we were viewing this scene from above, the throne would be in the middle of the heavenly throne room, surrounded by four living creatures who seem to guard the throne and offer perpetual worship to God. Encircling the throne are twenty-four thrones occupied by the twenty-four elders. Here, God's throne is associated with cosmic imagery, including lightning, thunder, rainbows, and the sea. If you are familiar with the traditional hymn "Holy, Holy, Holy," you might recall it mentions the "glassy sea" that lies before the throne of God. The important part of this image is that the sea is "glassy," or calm. Only flat, calm waters reflect in the same way glass does. It is helpful to remember that, throughout Scripture, the sea is a chaotic force, often associated with death. So when Jesus walks on water or calms the storm in the Gospels, it is a sign he has control over the chaotic and scary sea. The calm sea here functions similarly to remind us that God has control and that the sea is not a threat.

On the one hand, this heavenly throne room resembles the heavenly courts in some Hebrew Bible passages (cf. Ezekiel 1, Isaiah 6, Daniel 7). In 1 Kings 22:19, the prophet Micaiah recounts that he saw God seated on his throne with the whole host of heaven on his right and left. Psalm 82 also depicts God reigning as judge over a council of divine beings.[1] Similar to the author of the book of Job, John imagines God dwelling in a heavenly place and interacting with other heavenly beings (see Job 1:6–12, 2:1–7).[2] Isaiah 6 and Ezekiel 1 both describe God as seated on a heavenly throne surrounded by angels and other heavenly creatures. Lastly, Daniel 7:9 describes God as the "ancient of days," who occupies one of many thrones in heaven. In Daniel, the heavenly throne room is explicitly described as a courtroom where God sits in judgment over the earth.

John's first audience would have recalled these references in the Hebrew Bible, but they would have also recognized something in John's description of the heavenly throne room that was much closer

---

[1] For more information on Psalm 82 and the heavenly court, see Joshua T. James, *Psalms for Normal People: A Guide to the Most Relentlessly Theological Book in the Bible* (Harleysville, PA: The Bible for Normal People, 2023), 86–90.

[2] In the Job story, the angelic being, the Satan, is still part of God's entourage; he interacts with God and acts as God's agent. In Revelation, the Satan figure (now a dragon) will get thrown out of heaven, but we are getting ahead of ourselves!

to home: the imagery here reflects the very real political system of Rome. Ancient historians like Dio Cassius describe the Roman senate in remarkably similar terms to John's description of the heavenly throne room.[3] In Rome, the emperor's throne was placed in the middle of the room, with the chairs of the senators arranged around it in a semicircle. The Pantheon temple in Rome provides another good example of the kind of Roman architecture that John might have had in mind: a rounded room with a gap in the middle open to the heavens. Pantheon means something like "all gods," and statues of the gods were spaced around the walls of the room. We know that some emperors, like Hadrian, used it for certain government functions. By using this imagery, John is setting up a deliberate contrast between God's throne room and the emperor's, a contrast that will ultimately reveal God as the true sovereign and the emperor as a poor imitation of real power.

Roman senators wore white togas. Dio Cassius, our Roman historian, describes them with crowns that they threw to the ground as they bowed before the emperor in worship.[4] Sound familiar? The twenty-four elders in Revelation 4 are also dressed in white and wearing golden crowns, which they cast before God's throne when they worship and sing hymns of praise.

Such imagery would have been familiar to a first-century Christian, even if they didn't live in Rome. Crowns, white robes, throne-like chairs, and acts of worship all made up the political system of Rome where the emperor took center stage. These practices were reflected in the iconography and rituals of the provincial imperial cults in Asia Minor where similar acts of worship were offered to images of the emperor and other gods. What John reveals in his description of the heavenly throne room is that the heavenly court is not dissimilar to the earthly political court. He is therefore making not only a *theological*

---

[3] Dio Cassius, *Roman History*, 59.
[4] Dio Cassius, *Roman History*, 59.24.

statement about God's power but also a *political* one. Indeed, politics and religion in antiquity cannot be separated. They go hand in hand.

Describing the Divine (or Not)

God is described primarily as a jewel-encrusted thing of beauty in Revelation 4. The posture of being seated suggests God takes a human-like form, but no other human attributes are described. Instead, God looks like red jasper and orangey carnelian, both types of precious stones. Adding further color to the scene is an emerald rainbow that surrounds the throne and flashes of lightning that come from the throne. Thunder also rumbles from it.

As noted earlier, John appears to have combined a couple of Hebrew Bible passages in his description of God's heavenly throne room, but there are also points of contrast worth attending to. Like Ezekiel 1–3, this scene has flashes of light, the sound of thunder, and four living creatures around a throne. Ezekiel also describes the one seated on the throne as gleaming and colorful. However, unlike Ezekiel's depiction, the throne described by John doesn't move, but is fixed in place.

In Isaiah 6, the prophet sees God seated on a throne, the hem of his robe filling the temple. In that scene, God seems to wear human-like attire and is surrounded by seraphs. Compared with Isaiah, we can see that Revelation 4 minimizes the human aspects of God. There is no mention of clothing or anything anthropomorphic, such as the white hair on the figure depicted in Daniel 7. Rather, God is described in cosmic terms as something beyond human form.

Astonishingly, God does not speak in this scene (or very much at all in Revelation). The noise and activity happen around the throne, and God seems fixed in place like a spectacular piece of art that's so bright and brilliant one can barely look upon it. The effect of this on the reader is to give a sense of God as a still point, albeit a colorful and sparkling one, amidst a dramatic scene of heavenly worship.

So who else is in the scene?

God's Entourage

Powerful rulers come with an entourage, and the one around God's throne is rather spectacular. There are two groups that require a little bit of explanation. Let's begin with the twenty-four elders (4:4). Why there are twenty-four of them is a bit of a mystery, as this is not a typical biblical number. Scholars have various theories about who these twenty-four people are. The most likely theory is that twenty-four represents the twelve apostles and the twelve tribes of Israel. In other words, this is a group representing all those who have been faithful to God.

The elders' white robes could suggest purity or salvation, or they could indicate a political function. But in the text of Revelation, white robes have a specific purpose: they are given to those who conquer; that is, those who remain faithful to God despite hardship (3:4; 6:11; 7:9; 19:14). The elders' crowns support this imagery. In Greco-Roman culture, crowns were often given as a reward to victors in competitions. Revelation echoes this symbolism when the church in Smyrna is promised crowns if they conquer (2:10), and those in Philadelphia are threatened with the loss of their crowns if they don't "hold fast" (3:11). Like the white robes, crowns are one of God's reward to the faithful.

The twenty-four elders serve as a reminder of what awaits the faithful. After all, they are the only human creatures in a heavenly throne room full of angels and weird creatures. We might think of them as the first fruits of resurrection life. Additionally, they are the only ones to also have thrones, a promise made only to humans in Revelation. Just prior to this heavenly journey, the Son of Man has promised the congregation at Laodicea that those who conquer will be given a place on Jesus's throne (3:21).

The other cluster of characters around the throne are the four living creatures, or animals (the Greek word *zōon* could be translated as "animals," "creatures," or "living things"). They are never referred to as angels, although, like angels, they have wings. Nor are these typical animals. In any other context, we would describe them as monsters, for they are terrifying hybrid beings covered in eyes, with six wings apiece (4:8). One is like an ox, one like a lion, one like a human, and one like a flying eagle (4:7). There are various theories about the meaning of each animal. Some suggest they represent the four Gospel writers, who later Christians represented as a man (Matthew), a lion (Mark), an ox (Luke), and an eagle (John). This theory is highly unlikely, given the dating of these texts, and reflects an interpretation of this scene that began with Irenaeus in the second century CE.[5] Others point out the similarity between these living creatures and those in Ezekiel, and it is much more plausible that John drew on the imagery there. It is also noteworthy that many elements included in the Revelation 4 scene, including oxen and lions, are also depicted as statues and carvings in Solomon's temple (see 1 Kings 7:25, 29).

John seems to have adapted Ezekiel's living creatures, and one of the key changes he makes is that these creatures are "full of eyes in front and behind" (4:6, 8). Like the spirits before the throne, these creatures can see in all directions at once. We will look further at the significance of this later.

As the scene expands, we discover a third group around the throne. Typical of biblical and apocalyptic scenes of heaven, thousands and thousands of angels are also present (5:11). They join the twenty-four elders and four living creatures in praise. Taken as a whole, these various groups represent humans, the animal world, and the angelic host, all joined in unanimous praise of the divine. John tells us, "Then I heard every creature in heaven and on earth and under the earth and in the sea, and all that is in them, singing: 'To the one seated on the throne and to the Lamb be blessing and honor and glory and might forever and ever'" (5:13). This is nothing less than the whole created order praising God together.

---

[5] Revelation was likely written in the late first century CE, at least half a century before Irenaeus started writing about the Gospels in this way.

Enter the ~~Lion~~ Lamb (5:1–14)

After giving us an overview of the heavenly throne room, John directs our gaze back to the throne in the middle. Now he notices that God has a scroll. Like almost everything we will encounter in Revelation, this is not an ordinary scroll: it is written on both sides (inside and out) and is perfectly sealed with seven seals (5:1). Remember, seven is the number of completion, so this is the most sealed up a scroll can be. In antiquity, one usually only wrote on one side of a scroll, since the other side was too rough. This scroll is therefore both unusually chock full of writing and totally impenetrable. No wonder John weeps!

Who Is Worthy?

The key question in the scene in 5:1–14 is "who is worthy to open the scroll and break its seals?" (5:2). It is obviously important, yet no one on heaven or earth or even under the earth is found worthy to open this special, magical scroll. These three tiers—heaven, earth, and under the earth—reflect John's concept of the entire created order. It is a way of saying that God's angels searched the entire cosmos and were even prepared to descend to the realm of the dead (under the earth) to try to find someone worthy (5:3). In the end, God provides the solution.

An elder tells John not to weep, for the lion of the tribe of Judah was found worthy because he conquered (5:5). There is that conquering language again! Lions in the Bible represent strength and kingship, so we might expect to see a powerful lion who is like a royal Jewish warrior. Yet when John turns to look, he sees a lamb standing right by the throne, in the middle of the living creatures (5:6).

Jesus is only described as a lamb in Revelation and John's Gospel (John 1:29, 36), although the Greek word used is different in each text. In John's Gospel, Jesus is an *amnos* (lamb). In Revelation, Jesus is an *arnion*, a term we find in the Greek translation of Daniel 8:3

and 1 Enoch 90, where it is usually translated "ram."[6] The creature in Revelation is not a cute, fluffy little lamb skipping through green fields. Rather, it is a ram with seven horns and seven eyes—again, seven being the number of perfection or completeness—denoting complete power and an omnispective (all-seeing) gaze (5:6). So it's a ram with the attributes of that warrior lion we were expecting to see. For the sake of convention, I will refer to this image of Jesus as Lamb.

The Lamb is standing yet bears the marks of slaughter. John doesn't use the language of sacrifice (Greek: *thuō*) here but rather the language of murder (Greek: *sphazō*) to refer to the death of Jesus by the Roman state. It is the language of martyrdom rather than sacrificial atonement or Passover sacrifice. That is not to say John has no sense of atonement—he uses language of redemption and being freed from sins at several points (1:5; 5:9; 14:3–4)—but rather that it is not the dominant way he talks about Jesus's death. For John, the cross was the death of a faithful witness to God. Jesus's conquering of death is shown in his resurrection. (By the way, Luke's Gospel has a similar emphasis on the resurrection rather than the cross being the key event for salvation, but that is the topic for another book!)

That the Lamb is standing and alive symbolizes his resurrection; that he has seven heads and horns signifies his power. At several points in Revelation readers are reminded of Jesus's resurrected status (e.g. 1:18) and his status as ruler (e.g. 2:26–28; 12:5) precisely because they are important. The way John describes this is in the language of conquering: Jesus has conquered death and now rules with God. This is why he has the power to save. For this, the heavenly host that praised God in the previous scene now praise the Lamb, declaring him equally worthy of worship precisely because of his death and his overcoming of that death.

---

[6] The Greek translation of Daniel is part of the Septuagint (LXX), a translation of the Hebrew Bible roughly dating to the third to second centuries BCE. Most authors in the New Testament cite the Greek Septuagint when they cite the Hebrew Bible.

Worship

The key activity in the heavenly realm is worship, and worship serves to reinforce theology and identity. All the creatures around the throne face God and offer their praise (4:8–11). After the Lamb is revealed as worthy to open the scroll, he too is worshiped as equal to God (5:8–13). The scene culminates with Jesus and the enthroned God being worshiped by the entirety of the world who sing:

> To the one seated on the throne and to the Lamb
> be blessing and honor and glory and might
> forever and ever! (5:13)

Worship here consists of several parts—bowing down (obeisance/ Greek: *proskynesis*), singing hymns with musical accompaniment such as harps, and offering incense, which is a type of sacrifice. All of these are typical of worship in wider Greco-Roman culture. Hymns were sung in temple settings to pagan gods as well as to the emperor. The language we find in Revelation that proclaims God worthy of honor, glory, power, and blessing is typical for any ancient hymn to a deity or emperor. Likewise, people at this time offered sacrifices, including incense or non-animal burnt offerings, and they bowed before the gods or emperor.

Roman historian Dio Cassius records that the emperor Domitian was worshiped as "Lord and God."[7] As I mentioned earlier, he also writes that the senators used to pay obeisance (bow down) before the emperor's throne, offering sacrifices and casting their wreath-crowns upon the ground, much like the elders do in Revelation 4. Other ancient sources claim that the emperor Nero was applauded "day and night," and he was also referred to by the titles usually given to deities.[8] John is perhaps aware of these reports of the never-ceasing nature of

---

[7] Dio Cassius, *Roman History,* 67.4.7.
[8] Tacitus, *Annals,* 14.15.5.

imperial worship when he offers a glimpse of God receiving eternal worship. In contrast to earthly rulers, God is worshiped by the entire created order in an ongoing manner (5:13).

Why might worship be so important? One of the key themes in Revelation is about who you worship, because the object of your worship is a sign of your true allegiance. The main competition set up in the text is between worship of God (and the Lamb) and worship of the emperor and his idols. The heavenly worship described in Revelation 4–5 is the model for Christians to emulate. In contrast, we will also encounter scenes where people worship the beast, the dragon, or even the angels. Such worship is harshly condemned in the text as a way to reinforce that one must worship God alone.

Seeing and Being Seen

Did you notice all the eyes in the heavenly throne room? Eyes and sight are key themes in Revelation. As we've noted, John's commission is to "write what he sees," and the contents of the revelation are primarily communicated through sight, not speech. John wants us to notice this, and he repeatedly emphasizes that he is narrating what he sees.

> "I will show you…" (Jesus speaking to John, 4:1)
> And I saw… (5:1)
> And I saw… (5:2)
> Then I saw… (5:6)
> Then I saw… (5:11)

Sight was the primary way people engaged with their gods at the time John was writing. In wider Greco-Roman culture, worship happened in front of a visual representation of a deity. People would go to temples or other public places to make offerings before an image of a deity, placing incense, food, or some other gift at the base of a statue. Some people may also have had small altars and statues in their homes. In the large cities, cultic sites, like the altar to Zeus in Pergamum, were also set up for animal sacrifices to the gods. These altars functioned in much the same way they did in the temple in Jerusalem.

This wider cultural norm—that humans worship what they see—is reflected throughout Revelation, where worship happens in response to seeing something, such as a vision of the throne (4:10), the slaughtered Lamb (5:14), an image of the beast (13:15), an angel (19:1; 22:8), or an act of God (7:11; 11:16). Some of this worship is deemed idolatrous because the object is not God. John walks a fine line between reflecting (and sometimes critiquing) wider cultural norms and holding fast to more traditional Jewish sensibilities when it comes to the worship of God.

In the ancient world, Jewish religious practice differed from Greco-Roman religious traditions because the God known as YHWH[9] was not present via a statue, and Jewish tradition prohibited making an image of anything that could become an object of worship (see Exodus 20:4–5). In this sense, Jews were profoundly countercultural. This did not mean, however, that they did not yearn to see God.

In Revelation we get a sense of people's yearning to see God, continuing a thread that weaves its way throughout the Hebrew Bible. When surrounded by cultures that worship deities they can see, God's people also seek this kind of interaction with their God. Seeing God means intimacy with God. To be face-to-face with God means being profoundly intimate with the divine. In Revelation, one of the final promises of the book is that humans "will see God's face" in the New Jerusalem (22:4). This is a good thing! God's face is associated with blessing and favor.[10] The blessing in Numbers 6:24–26 expresses it as

---

[9] YHWH are the consonants (tetragrammaton) for the Hebrew name for God revealed to Moses in Exodus 6:2–3. Out of respect for God's name it is not pronounced. Where this name occurs in the text, many English-language Bibles denote it with LORD (all capitals).

[10] Earlier, we noted that God's face is also associated with God's wrath and judgment (Revelation 6:16). These two aspects are held in tension in the book, as they are in the Hebrew Bible.

follows: "The LORD bless you and keep you, the LORD shine his face upon you and be gracious to you, the LORD lift up his countenance upon you, and give you peace." Conversely, God turning away God's face is synonymous with the withdrawal of divine presence (Deuteronomy 31:17).

But the biblical tradition is also complicated when it comes to seeing God. Moses asks to see God and is only allowed a glimpse of God's back because "no one can see me [God] and live" (Exodus 33:18–20). Isaiah, Jacob, Gideon, Ezekiel, and Elijah all express fear at the prospect of seeing God because of this association with death. As noted in the previous chapter, this tradition lies behind John falling as though dead when he turns and sees the risen Christ (Revelation 1:17).

Seeing God is dangerous, and these Hebrew Bible texts suggest God *can* be seen. God has a form. But perhaps this fear of actually seeing God is one of the reasons John only describes the one seated on the throne through symbols that give a general effect. Yet, despite this fear of seeing God, John vividly narrates the details of the heavenly throne room and everything that flows out of it in the chapters that follow. He does so in a way that invites us to see with him, allowing us to imagine this scene almost as if we were there. The effect is to bridge the gap between God and the reader, helping us get a glimpse of God via John's words.

Seeing in Revelation, however, is a two-way process. When we look at God in this text, we readers find ourselves looking at a God who is looking right back at us. Is this comforting? Perhaps. Terrifying? Definitely. But it is also important.

God's gaze is made evident in several ways in the vision conveyed in Revelation 4–5. Directly around the throne are:

- "seven flaming torches, which are the seven spirits of God" (4:5; they're also the Lamb's eyes—I'll explain shortly);
- "living creatures, *full of eyes in front and behind*" (4:6);
- "four living creatures, [which] are *full of eyes all around and inside*" (4:8);

- "a Lamb standing as if it had been slaughtered, having seven horns and seven eyes, which are the seven spirits of God *sent out into all the earth*" (5:6).

Notice how many sevens there are—remember, seven is the number of completeness or perfection. The Lamb has seven eyes which, John tells us, are also the seven flame-spirits sent forth by God. God and Jesus share this symbol, one that suggests a perfectly seeing deity. These eye-spirits roam the earth, making God's perfect vision also all-pervasive. Those who grew up in conservative Christian circles might remember the fear that came from being told (or warned) by their parents that Jesus saw everything, even things done in secret! Just like my own parents, John wants his audience to know that ***God is watching***.

The sense of God's all-pervasive gaze is also communicated through the living creatures being full of eyes inside and around. They can see in all directions and, if lots of eyes mean a lot of seeing, they can see *a lot*. God therefore has supernatural spies who are also guarding the throne and watching the world.

In the last chapter we noted that the opening vision of Christ was a way of letting Christians know Jesus was present and in their midst. In a similar way, this vision in Revelation 4–5 lets readers know that God sees their pain and their struggle. God knows what is happening on earth, and God is about to do something about it. That process begins with the four horsemen of the apocalypse in the very next chapter.

Confused Yet?

We began this chapter noting that the dense symbolism of John's visions can be challenging, disturbing, and discombobulating. So what is the point? When we readers get to glimpse the shining, colorful, glorious, moving spectacle that is the heavenly throne room, I think we are supposed to be awed by its beauty and inspired to worship. We are getting to see the God who might feel distant but is made nearer through our imaginations.

There is much that is familiar about the way John describes the divine. God is ruling as an all-powerful, all-seeing deity surrounded by a heavenly court. Jesus is there too, but he is a bit more confronting, for he is both a vulnerable, wounded Lamb and the all-powerful warrior Lion-Ram. This tension, between Jesus as conquering warrior *and* as willing martyr, runs throughout Revelation. We don't get to pick just one Jesus. If Jesus is victor, he is also a victim, and vice versa. Lastly, comfort is offered in the image of the twenty-four elders who worship God, a foretaste of future resurrected life for faithful humans.

Ultimately, I think John wants us to leave this scene knowing that, first, God is ruling in heaven, and second, God sees everything and is well aware of what is happening on earth. What God does in response, comes next.

CHAPTER FOUR

Judgment

In Revelation 6 the scene moves from heavenly worship to chapters and chapters of judgments that unfold in three series of seven: seven seals, seven trumpets, and seven bowls unleash judgment upon the earth. In between some of these judgments we get interludes—brief breaks—where John's vision shifts back to the heavenly realm, or to another time, to describe something else. As we navigate this portion of the text, there are several questions that emerge. Why judgment? Why is God angry? At whom is God's wrath directed? What do we do with all the violence? And what exactly is being imagined here—something that has happened, that will happen, or is this simply wishful thinking from the author?

Table 1 presents the three sets of seven judgments alongside one another. This allows us to see their shared themes as well as their variety and contradictions. If we were to read these chapters as descriptions of literal or chronological events (which I don't think they are), then the earth would be destroyed several times over. The numbers just don't add up! But as prophetic rhetoric designed to remind readers to stay faithful to God, John's descriptions of judgment are effective. You do not want to be on God's bad side.

JUDGMENTS	SEVEN SEALS 6:1–8:1	SEVEN TRUMPETS 8:2–11:19	SEVEN BOWLS 15:1–16:21
	The Lamb opens the seals	Seven angels blow trumpets	Seven angels pour out bowls of seven plagues
1st	Rider of the white horse: "conquers"	A third of the earth is destroyed with hail, fire, and blood	Painful sores are inflicted on followers of the beast
2nd	Rider of the red horse: takes away peace	A third of the sea dies	The sea turns to blood, everything dies
3rd	Rider of the black horse: crops are destroyed	A third of the waters become bitter (Wormwood)	Rivers and springs turn to blood
4th	Rider of the pale green horse: a quarter of the people of the earth are killed	A third of the sun, moon, and stars are darkened	The sun scorches the earth
5th	The saints cry out for vengeance	Star falls to earth and opens the pit: locusts torture unsealed people	The beast's kingdom is in darkness; people suffer painful sores
6th	There is an earthquake, and darkness covers the earth	A third of humanity is killed by four angels and their horsemen	The Euphrates dries up; an army assembles at Armageddon
Interlude	144,000 faithful servants receive God's seal of protection	A mighty angel gives John a little scroll to eat Two witnesses measure the temple	
7th	There is silence in heaven	Heaven praises God The Ark of the Covenant is opened	There is a violent earthquake and a plague of hailstones
Interlude		The dragon and his beasts are thrown to earth The Son of Man harvests the earth	

The Seven Seals (6:1–8:1)

As the scene of heavenly worship ends with the elders falling and worshiping the Lamb, John writes the following:

> Then I saw the Lamb open one of the seven seals, and I heard one of the four living creatures call out as with a voice of thunder: "go." I looked, and there was a white horse. Its rider had a bow, a crown was given to him, and he came out conquering and to conquer. (6:1–2)

In chapter three, I mentioned there was much anxiety in heaven over who could open the sealed scroll (5:2–4). This anxiety suggests the contents are vitally important, yet readers of Revelation do not get much warning about their nature. As each of the seals is broken, the appearance of peace and stability on earth is systematically undone: peace is taken, causing people to kill one another; grain crops are destroyed, leading to a failure of the food economy; a quarter of the earth's inhabitants are destroyed; martyrs cry out for vengeance; and the whole earth, from kings to enslaved people, are so terrified that they cry to the mountains, "fall on us and hide us from the face of the one seated upon the throne and from the wrath of the Lamb" (6:16). Maybe it would have been better for the scroll to stay sealed?

The Four Horsemen

The four horsemen of the apocalypse are one set of symbols in Revelation that have a long reception history. Made famous by the print artist Albrecht Dürer, who depicted them riding out as a group in his *Apocalypse* woodcuts (circa 1498), these four horsemen have come to be a symbol of impending doom.

The identity of the first horseman is the most controversial. The horse is white, and the rider wears the crown of victory, leading some to suggest he is a Christ figure (see the later Christ rider in Revelation

19:11) and others to claim he's a satanic figure. Either way, the rider emerges and is commanded from heaven, implying God is in control and issuing the orders here. The next three riders are more clearly agents of destruction, although they too ride out from the heavenly realm.

John, as narrator, is still up in heaven, so he's able to see and hear the living creatures issue the command to come/go (the Greek word *erchomai* can convey either meaning).[1] Each horse has its own color and their riders perform actions that make them stand out from the usual cavalry. Nevertheless, the four riders share certain features with the types of military horsemen found in the surrounding regions. Just as the rider of the white horse carries a bow, so too did the Assyrian and Babylonian armies use mounted archers to conquer Judea, and the mounted archers of the Parthians were a constant threat to Rome's eastern border. Roman riders wore swords like the rider of the red horse, so John appears to draw upon the fear of Rome's military might in his use of this image. The rider of the black horse carries scales and is linked to the heightened cost of food and the pale green horse brings death in all its forms. For people living in this era, it would not have been a challenge to imagine cavalry decimating crops and ending lives.

As well as alluding to familiar military images, John appears to be rewriting and updating Zechariah here, drawing upon the horses that patrol the earth in Zechariah 1:8–11 (see also the chariots in Zechariah 6:1–8 with their red, white, gray, and black horses). In Zechariah 1, the horses are red, orange-ish, and white in color (1:8). Their job is to patrol the earth, and they report back to the angel of the Lord that the earth is at peace (1:10–11). But this is not the good news it might seem, for a peaceful earth means that the people of Jerusalem and Judea are still under foreign rule. The angel of the Lord cries out to God, asking

---

[1] The NRSV and most major translations traditionally have "come" as the command. Yet the narrative describes something moving from the heavenly realm onto the earth, making "go" a more plausible translation of the command. This also fits with the military nature of the image, where the commander instructs the cavalry to ride out.

how long mercy will be withheld from these people. In response, God promises to return to Jerusalem, bringing both compassion and a measuring line that will be stretched across the city—a sign that it will be rebuilt (1:16–17). Later in Zechariah, God also promises to return like lightning, sounding the trumpet and marching forth to destroy the enemies of God's covenant people (9:14–16).

By utilizing the prophecies from Zechariah in the way he depicts the four horsemen, John is framing this vision of God's judgments in Revelation 6 as the fulfillment of God's promised mercy and justice. A similar refrain to the angel's cry in Zechariah 1:12 now occurs in the mouths of the martyrs hiding under the heavenly altar. They are revealed when the fifth seal is broken, and they cry out, "how long, O Holy and True Despot,[2] will you not judge and avenge our blood from the inhabitants of the earth?" (6:10).

Destabilizing *Pax Romana*

The judgments that fall over the earth in Revelation 6 increase in seriousness. Each time, the images John describes work to destabilize any notion of the earth as peaceful, stable, prosperous, or just. It is important to note the historical context here. The Roman Empire was widely credited with bringing peace, stability, and abundance to the region through its military might and economic prosperity. In Latin, this is referred to as the *Pax Romana*—the peace of Rome.

Along with military power, the emperor controlled the distribution of grain, including setting the prices for those in the provinces who were farming grain for the empire. The fact that there were various peasant uprisings during the first century CE suggests this was not always perceived as a happy or fair relationship. When food was in

---

[2] The Greek word I've translated "Despot" is *despotēs* which means absolute ruler. It is often translated "Sovereign Lord" in English Bibles but I've kept Despot here because it captures the sense of dominance in the title John uses for God.

short supply, priority was given to feeding the army and the elites in Rome. The prices cited in Revelation 6:6 reflect the effect on the poor of such economic disparity—these prices are about eight to fifteen times higher than normal and would therefore put everyday grain like wheat and barley beyond the reach of the average person.

Imperial oppression and food shortages were not the only challenges for those living under Roman rule. While the Roman Empire was known for its technological advances and sewerage systems, infectious diseases were still incredibly dangerous. The rider of the pale green horse brings not only famine and war but also that other great killer in antiquity—disease. Together, the horsemen represent war, disease, hunger, and economic dysfunction coming to earth. These are not future events, but lived realities for inhabitants of the Roman Empire during the first century CE. John takes these ordinary realities and subverts them, portraying them as signs of God's judgment against the empire.

The Apocalyptic Wrath of God

When the sixth seal opens (6:12), the outcome is different to what has preceded, because the threat is no longer of human making (e.g., disease, war, inequity). John describes more typical apocalyptic signs of judgment and the End: there is an earthquake, the sun becomes black, the moon is like blood, stars fall, seasonal chaos means the fruit trees lose fruit, and the whole natural world, as well as the heavens, seem to shake and move (6:12–14). Here we get the first mention of what might be behind these events—the wrath of God, or more specifically, the wrath of the Lamb (6:16).

Divine wrath, or anger, can be a problematic idea for many contemporary Christians, in part because it is often misappropriated—and therefore misunderstood—in our modern world. The first thing to note here is that these verses describe God's actions and God's anger (not human action or revenge). John is drawing on a Hebrew Bible tradition of the "day of wrath" as a day of reckoning. This tradition is evoked particularly in response to the destruction of Jerusalem in 586/7 BCE, but it also refers more generally to God's judgment of sin and correction of injustice (Job 21:30; Zephaniah 1:15; cf. Romans 2:5; Ephesians 5:6). So we have to keep reading to discover why God is so angry in Revelation.

Divine wrath in this part of Revelation is directed at the nations and also, more specifically, at all who worshiped the beast or any idol. Both of these objects of divine wrath are familiar from the Hebrew Bible, and John positions himself as a prophet in this tradition.[3] God's wrath is directed toward those who would destroy his earth (11:18, 19:15), kill his covenant people (16:19), and practice idolatry (14:8–10).

Earthly status offers no protection against the judgment described in Revelation 6: John tells us that he sees kings, magnates, generals, the rich, the powerful, the enslaved, and the free *all* running for their lives (6:15). The message is that no amount of human status or wealth can protect you from the wrath of God. There is a way to be protected, and that is with God's seal. We'll meet those protected people next.

144,000

Between the opening of the sixth and seventh seals, we readers of Revelation are given a brief hiatus from the violence. Four angels hold back any further threat to human life to allow "the servants [or enslaved people] of our God" to have a seal placed on their foreheads (7:1–3). The language of seal (Greek: *sphragis*) suggests something like an imprint made to press into wax, such as a ring or royal inscription. God is effectively signing the foreheads of his servants (see 14:1), marking them as his own, perhaps in a dual allusion to both baptism and the practice of enslavers branding those they had enslaved. I recognize

---

[3] Hebrew Bible examples of divine anger against the nations can be found in Amos 1:1–2:3; Isaiah 47; and Ezekiel 25–31. For judgment of idolatry see Ezekiel 16 and 23; Hosea 1–3; and Jeremiah 10:1–10.

this latter image is horrific, but it would have been all too common a sight at this time. Moreover, the language John uses for this group is "servants/enslaved people of God" (the Greek word *doulos* can be translated "servant" or "enslaved person").

The quantity of those sealed is the famous number 144,000. We meet this group twice in Revelation, here and in 14:1–5. John is playing with numbers again, using multiples of twelve, based upon the twelve tribes of Israel, to depict a huge crowd. In some traditions, 144,000 is taken as the literal limit to the number of people who can reign with God. Certainly, in 14:1–5, this group seems to have a special status, because only they can learn the "new song" that is sung before the throne. However, their special status is as first-fruits, not exclusive fruits (14:4). They serve as a hopeful reminder that faithfulness to God will be rewarded and that a place has been prepared on Mount Zion, the mountain to which all the nations stream in prophetic images of God's redemption (see Isaiah 2:2–3; Micah 4:1–2).

We can see John's concern with purity in his description of the 144,000. They are not only representatives of the twelve tribes of Israel but also of those "who have not defiled themselves with women, for they are virgins" (NRSV 14:4). The Greek word *parthenoi* (singular *parthenos*) is often translated as "virgins," but that does not fully capture the word's meaning; *parthenos* literally means "unmarried girl." So the 144,000 are supposedly men who have not "defiled themselves" with women, but they are also described as unmarried girls. John appears to subvert and expand traditional gender categories in the way he imagines the gender of this group.[4] But what is particularly interesting is the way John emphasizes their sexual purity to make a point about their faithfulness to the Lamb. As we have already seen, John draws upon the language of sexual purity to describe religious fidelity.

---

[4] Lynn R. Huber, "Gazing at the Whore: Reading Revelation Queerly," in *Bible Trouble: Queer Reading at the Boundaries of Biblical Scholarship*, ed. Teresa J. Hornsby and Ken Stone (Semeia Studies 67; Atlanta: SBL Press, 2011), 301–20 (p. 317).

The interlude in Revelation 7 also introduces another group—a "great multitude" of people from every nation and language (7:9). Their white robes symbolize holiness or purity, and the palm branches they are holding represent victory. When questioned by an elder about the group's identity, John responds that the elder already knows. This elder replies that the group represents those who have survived an ordeal and remained faithful. They symbolize an expanded and more diverse group of God's faithful people, who join the 144,000 to worship God and receive God's promise that they will live in peace.

Summing Up the Seven Seals

The first series of judgments begins a section of Revelation that reveals God's wrath against idol worshipers and those who would destroy God's people and earth. By moving between descriptions of the judgments and scenes of redeemed people living in peace and worshiping God, John juxtaposes the realities of heaven, or God's reign, and earth, Rome's reign. John reveals the fragility of the *Pax Romana* by describing the world's conflict, death, famine, and suffering. He is yet again laying out two choices for his readers: team God or team world.

The series of seven seals ends with a long silence in the heavenly realm (8:1). In context, the silence here makes most sense as a profound moment of awe in the face of God's action. It is the silence of worship and prayer. Worship punctuates these visions, often serving to confirm, affirm, or give a reason for the judgment. At the beginning of Revelation 8, an angel brings the prayers of the saints to the heavenly altar, offering them alongside the incense offering. This short scene of worship gives readers a rationale for the trumpet blasts that will soon sound from heaven: God is responding to the pleas of God's people for justice and vengeance. The earlier cry of "how long, O Lord?" (6:10) continues to echo across these judgments.

Seven Trumpets (8:2–11:19)

The series of seven trumpets has a bit more internal consistency compared with the other two series of judgments. Each time an angel sounds their trumpet, a third of something is destroyed—people, waters, skies, plants, and so on. Like the first series, there is an interlude between the sixth and seventh blast. This time, though, the interlude is much longer and gives an explanation for the delay in God's judgment.

This series of seven judgments shares several features with the first. Both use images that suggest war, and both allude to cosmic upset and the loss of human life. In many ways, it is the same story being told with a bit of variation. The new features in this series are the star called Wormwood, the demonic locusts, and the destroying angels, so we will take a brief look at each of these in turn.

At the third trumpet blast, a great star falls into the waters of the earth (Revelation 8:10–12). In antiquity, falling stars or comets were sometimes read as signs of death or some other gloomy portent, or they could represent angelic figures. This star has a name, Wormwood, which is otherwise not mentioned in the biblical tradition. The Greek for Wormwood is *apsinthion*, which is a bitter plant used in ancient medicine, and this is the imagery John uses here. With absinthe, water becomes undrinkable and even poisoned due to its bitterness.

The fifth trumpet blast introduces a second falling star (9:1–2). This star is most likely an angelic figure who is able to open the bottomless pit, a term that suggests a dark, hell-like place under the earth (Greek: *abyss*). We will discuss that concept more fully in chapter seven. It is worth noting that stars and angels are sometimes treated interchangeably in Jewish and apocalyptic texts (e.g., Job 38:7; Judges 5:20) and the metaphor of falling stars was used to denote fallen angels (Isaiah 14:12; Luke 10:18). It is unclear whether this particular angel has been sent to do a job or is a fallen (bad) angel, such as the dragon we will meet in Revelation 12. Either way, he serves God's purpose by unleashing terrifying, demonic horse-like locusts, who torture those without God's seal on their forehead over a period of five months (9:3–5). The humans sealed with God's seal are protected and are not harmed by the locusts. Next, we meet another angel who is described as the king of the pit, and he serves as a reminder that angels can be both good *and* evil. We are told that this angel's name is Abaddon ("destruction") in Hebrew and Apollyon ("destroyer") in Greek (9:11); John is making sure that both Hebrew and Greek speakers understand this angel brings death, not life.

The last new feature in this series of judgments is a group of four angels released by the sixth trumpet blast (9:13ff). They are a reminder that angels are not pretty white creatures with fluffy wings; rather, they are capable of absolute destruction. These angels kill a third of humanity and do so by sending a monstrous cavalry. Like the demonic locusts in 9:3–5, these are not normal horses. They have heads like lions, fire-breathing mouths, and tails that sting like scorpions. There are also unfathomable numbers of them (9:16).

Despite painting a picture of utter terror, John claims that the survivors of these horrors "did not repent of the works of their hands, in that they did not stop worshiping demons and idols" (9:20). Idolatry is again front and center as one of John's main concerns. This time, he adds other sins to the list (9:21), implying that they are being judged not only because they are idolatrous, but also because they are murderers, sorcerers, and thieves, as well as being sexually immoral (or perhaps, religiously unfaithful). All three lists of bad behaviors in Revelation include murder, immorality, sorcery (magic), and idolatry (see 9:20–21, 21:8; 22:15), while lying and thieving are occasionally included too. These are fairly standard vices in ancient sources and a stereotypical way of suggesting one's enemies are utterly morally corrupt.

The Two Witnesses (11:1–14)

Before the seventh trumpet blasts, we get a long interlude that interrupts the narrative. First, there is another vision of a mighty angel, who again commissions John and asks him to eat a little scroll (10:1–11).

This is a reaffirmation of his prophetic call, one that evokes the tradition in Ezekiel 2:8–3:3.

The more interesting, and also more confusing, part of this interlude is the scene involving two witnesses (11:1–19). The scene starts with John being told to measure the temple, a motif we find in several other apocalyptic texts (1 Enoch 61; Zecheriah 2:1–2; Ezekiel 40:3). Up to this point in Revelation, John has been an observer, writing down what he sees. Now he must participate. This task of measuring the temple evokes Zechariah 2 and Ezekiel 40–42, but it also serves to introduce a period of time when the holy city of Jerusalem is "given over to the nations" (11:2). This period is forty-two months, or three and a half years.

Forty-two months, or three and a half years, is also the same as 1260 days (11:3). These sets of numbers appear several times in this section of Revelation, suggesting they are important. In Daniel, it is the length of time that the Jewish community lives under foreign oppression (Daniel 12:7). This specified timespan works in two ways. On the one hand, it is a reminder to those who are suffering that their distress will not last for very long because God will put an end to it. On the other hand, the period of delay before God's judgment allows people to repent. In other words, it is a way to offer mercy to those who do not yet believe. This latter reason relates to the role of the two witnesses.

While shrouded in rather strange imagery, the two witnesses are basically two prophetic figures capable of performing signs to witness for God. They will die for their witness, as is often the case in Revelation, becoming martyrs for the cause (11:7). John thus locates them in the wider biblical traditions of prophets who are killed by the opponents of God (1 Kings 18:3–4; 2 Chronicles 24:20–21; Luke 13:34). The witnesses' lack of a proper burial is doubly shameful, as their bodies will be left in the street (11:8). But that is not the end of the story. After three and a half days, God will raise them as a sign of hope in the resurrection (11:7–11). You'll notice that the period of time here is the same as the one mentioned earlier, but now it is expressed in days rather than years. It is a reminder that these references to time are working at a symbolic level.

The witnesses' resurrection in 11:11 is described as a type of re-creation. God breathes life into them, much like God did to Adam in Genesis 2:7, reanimating the witnesses' dead bodies. It is a reminder of the power of God and it evokes terror in those who see them stand up and ascend to heaven in a cloud. The witnesses are also a symbol of the church. They do what John wants the Christian communities in Asia Minor to do: witness to God, even if it means risking their lives, in the knowledge that God will restore them in the end.

The Seventh Trumpet (11:15–19)

More earthquakes shake the world before, finally, the seventh trumpet is sounded (11:13–15). When it is, heaven worships by singing hymns of praise to God. This parallels the silence of worship when the seventh seal is opened. There is a deeper resonance in these patterns of seven and the role of worship. Just as God rested on the seventh day of creation and the sabbath became a day for rest and worship in the Jewish tradition, so the seventh seal/trumpet leads to worship and rest instead of work or activity. Furthermore, the vision of heavenly worship reveals the Ark of the Covenant is there in heaven (11:19). This is the Ark that disappeared when the first Jerusalem temple was destroyed by the invading Babylonian army in 587 BCE. What was thought to be lost has been kept in heaven. It is yet another reminder of how deeply Jewish this author is in his worldview, and how his thinking is steeped in the imagery and teachings of the Hebrew Bible.

The Seven Bowls of Plagues (15:1–16:21)

The last series of judgments comes in the form of seven angels pouring out seven bowls. (We have skipped Revelation 12–13 because I will address them more fully in the next chapter.) Again, these judgments are framed by worship from the heavenly realm. The servants of God sing a song to God and the Lamb, proclaiming their judgments as "righteous and true" and declaring to them that, because of God's judgment, "all the nations will come and bow down (worship) before you" (15:2–4). That is, judgment is not just to prove God's might or to seek vengeance. Witnessing to God's judgment is supposed to lead people to repentance and, ultimately, to worship God.

The seven bowls are called the seven plagues in 15:6. You might already have noticed some resonances between the kinds of judgments unleashed in Revelation and the plagues in Exodus (sores, water turned to blood). This connection becomes much clearer in the final series of judgments. Not only does John use the language of "plagues" to refer to what comes out of the bowls, but the pattern of events resembles those described in Exodus 7–12. Yet again, John seems to be drawing upon biblical traditions, this time to make connections between God's judgment on injustice and the need for liberation and justice for God's people. In the table below I have listed the plagues in Exodus against similar "plagues" in the judgment scenes in Revelation. While these parallels are concentrated in the bowl series, we find at least one in the trumpet series, too.

PLAGUES IN EXODUS	PLAGUES IN REVELATION
The Nile is turned to blood / fish die (7:14–24)	Second and third bowls: water and sea turned to blood, fish die (16:3–4)
Frogs (8:1–15)	Sixth bowl: demonic frogs (16:13–15)
Festering boils (9:8–12)	First bowl: foul sores (16:2)
Hail and fire destroy plants and animals (9:13–35)	Seventh bowl: hail (16:20–21)
Locusts (10:1–20)	Fifth trumpet: demonic locusts (9:1–11)
Darkness (10:21–23)	Fifth bowl: darkness over land (16:10)
Passover lamb's blood as protection (12:1–30)	Fifth trumpet: God's seal as protection (9:4)

While the order of the plagues is different, perhaps because John is relying on memory, we can see that the plagues of Exodus are most strongly reflected in this last series of judgments relating to the seven bowls. John has upped the ante though, turning regular locusts and frogs into demonic monster versions. Everything is bigger and more terrifying in Revelation. Even the earthquake is the most violent that anyone has ever experienced on earth (16:18).

Much like the narrative in Exodus, the refrain "they did not repent" punctuates the judgment in Revelation 16 at regular intervals (16:9, 11); this is juxtaposed with the assertion from the heavenly choir that God's judgments are just. As before, the targets of the judgment are those who have "the mark of the beast and who worship its icon" (16:2).

Armageddon

A popular interpretation of Revelation is that this book predicts a final great battle in a place known as Armageddon. There are various theories about this: in the 1980s, it was interpreted as a prediction of nuclear war with Russia; now it is usually associated with notions of a final war in the Middle East.[5] The name Armageddon has become so synonymous with the idea of utter apocalyptic destruction that there is even a film called *Armageddon* (1998), starring Bruce Willis and Ben Affleck, where the world is threatened with destruction by a meteor. Most of these theories about Armageddon are the result of a massive over-translation of a few verses.

Revelation 16:16 is the only place in the New Testament that mentions Armageddon. There have been various attempts to identify the precise location of Armageddon,[6] but we are not in the realm of

---

[5] Hal Lindsey's *The Late Great Planet Earth* (Zondervan, 1970) popularized these types of interpretations that linked Revelation with current events.
[6] The word could be the Greek version of the Hebrew, *Har Megiddo* (Mount Megiddo), and some have suggested this is the location John intends. However,

literalism here, and trying to locate a precise time and place for this war is not the point of John's allusion. The creatures assembling at Armageddon in the book of Revelation are three spirit-frogs, who come from the mouth of the dragon and gather an army of kings from the "whole world." Other apocalyptic texts also refer to a final battle, where God's enemies assemble against God (see Ezekiel 38–39; 1 Enoch 56:5–7; 4 Ezra 13:34–35; Sibylline Oracles 3).[7] These enemies might be either human beings or supernatural beings like angels. By using this symbolism, John conveys a sense that opposition to God's people seems to be increasing *and* feels immense (encompassing the whole world!). He also points out that this is the result of evil spirits associated with the dragon. When God destroys the dragon, which happens soon, such threats will also be destroyed.

What Is with the Judgments?

As the three series of seven judgments have unfolded, a few themes have emerged. The first is that the judgments become more dramatic with each telling. Despite this, the followers of the beast do not repent. Second, the judgments of God are framed by worship and are issued from the heavenly temple: the seals are broken by the Lamb on the throne; the trumpets are sounded by angels in heaven; and the bowls are liturgical vessels that hold incense for the heavenly altar. Justice and worship are intertwined in John's theology. In modern terms, John is saying that worship is not something that stays within the walls of the church. In John's theology, the songs and rituals enact a worldview that

---

Megiddo in northern Israel is not a mountain or even a hill, and the spelling differs so I am not convinced he had that particular location in mind.

[7] 4 Ezra is Jewish apocalypse dated to the first century CE like Revelation. The Sibylline Oracles are a collection of prophetic oracles written in Greek that contain apocalyptic elements. They were probably composed by Jews, and while dating them is difficult, some were likely composed in the first century BCE.

results in real world-changing action. To sing these words and neither witness to God nor act for justice is a disconnect that John cannot imagine.

The third aspect we can trace in these chapters is that the target of the judgments becomes more specific. In the first series, God judges idolatry and general immorality (murderers, thieves, etc.). By the time we reach Revelation 16, the plagues are directed specifically at those who worship the beast's icon and have his mark. The beast was revealed in the interlude just prior to the final series of seven judgments (we skipped over these chapters), and we turn to them now to unpack who this beast is and why John (or God) really doesn't like him.

CHAPTER FIVE

Here Comes the Dragon

The way John has structured Revelation means we encounter numerous visions of the divine long before we meet any evil characters. So far, readers have been invited to "see" with John the risen Christ who appears as the bright and terrifying Son of Man (1:12–20), the enthroned deity surrounded by a great entourage of heavenly creatures and cosmic symbols (4:1–8), and the Ram-Lamb, who is multi-headed and multi-horned with eyes that roam the earth (5:6–8). These divine beings are praised by the whole of heaven; their reign is announced, and they issue judgments over the earth. These scenes act to establish God's rule and power, so that when we meet the antagonists we will recognize they are but poor imitations of the true ruler of the world.

In the second half of Revelation, the scenes of conflict between God and evil increase, and we start to get detailed and specific descriptions of this evil. We don't meet personifications of the forces that oppose God until chapter 12. When we do, they are rather spectacular, coming to us in the forms of a great multi-headed dragon, two bizarre beasts, and a beautiful but blood-thirsty prostitute who appears riding the dragon (who we will discuss in the next chapter). We will look at each of these ways of symbolizing evil, asking how their symbolism might have been understood in the first century CE, why John might have depicted them in the way he did, and what function they play in the text.

The Dragon (12:1–18)

Revelation 12 begins with John announcing that a "great sign" appeared in the heavens (or sky).[1] This sign is a pregnant woman clothed with the sun, moon, and stars. This description presents her as a kind of goddess, someone more than human, suggesting the child she carries is someone important—the son of a deity. Many scholars think she represents the Christian church or perhaps Mary, Jesus's mother. We'll return to her in a moment, but let's start with the next sign: "a great red dragon having seven heads and ten horns and seven diadems on his heads" (12:3).

Dragon, Ancient Serpent, Devil, Satan

In Revelation, evil is presented and embodied as a great multi-headed dragon monster. John describes this creature using a variety of terms: "the great dragon was thrown down, that ancient serpent, who is called the Devil and Satan, the deceiver of the whole world" (12:9). We see here a cluster of names, as well as mythologies, being invoked to describe the great red dragon. Let's begin with the names.

The term for dragon (Greek: *drakōn*) only appears here in the New Testament. Dragons are more dominant in Greek mythology than in the biblical tradition: Hydra, Python, and Typhon are just three of the monsters in Greek tradition who are described as either red or multi-headed. We have hints of these kinds of monsters in the Hebrew Bible's references to Leviathan, who is referred to as a *drakōn* in the Greek translation of Job 41:1 (LXX 40:25), Psalm 74:13 (LXX 73:13),[2] and Isaiah 27:1. The red dragon in Revelation 12 is clearly powerful, as

---

[1] The Greek word *ouranos* can mean sky or heaven (in the sense of another realm we can't see). Here it has the sense of sky.
[2] LXX here refers to the Greek translation of the Hebrew Bible, the Septuagint. At several points the chapters and verses don't quite line up, hence the two sets of numbers.

indicated by his multiple heads and horns, his diadems, and the fact that his tail is able to sweep a third of the stars from heaven (12:4). Diadems are a bit like crowns, but the Greek word (*diadēmata*) is different to that used for the crowns (*stephanoi*) the elders wear in heaven (4:4, 10) or those promised to the faithful (2:10). These *stephanoi* crowns are more like wreaths, which are given as rewards for victory in games or war. Diadems, on the other hand, are worn by royalty in Persia, suggesting they are associated with rulers. Only the dragon, the beast, and the Christ rider wear diadems in Revelation (12:3; 13:1; 19:12). The dragon has seven of them (the perfect number), the beast wears ten, and Christ has "many." Just in case it's not obvious, that means Christ wins because he has the most. These numbers matter!

The dragon is also named as "that ancient serpent." Snakes are often associated with threat and death in the Bible (Exodus 7:10; Deuteronomy 32:33), but this serpent is most likely a specific reference to Genesis 3. In that story, the serpent talked Adam and Eve into disobeying God in the garden of Eden. Deceiving people to do the opposite of what God wants is one of the key traits of evil in Revelation. All the "bad" characters in Revelation deceive: Jezebel and other false prophets deceive Jesus's followers to practice idolatry or make images to worship (2:20; 12:9; 13:14; 19:20), and the beasts, or Rome, deceive "the nations" (18:23; 20:3, 8–10). John tells us that this dragon-serpent is "the deceiver of the whole world" (12:9).

John calls the dragon both Devil (Greek: *diabolos*) and Satan (Greek: *satanas*), and in doing so combines two traditions. The first is the name for an evil figure in the Greek translation of the Hebrew Bible, where *diabolos* is "the slanderer." The second name, "Satan," is only found in Jewish texts such as the Hebrew Bible and later Jewish apocalypses where it is usually not a name at all, but a role title—"the satan" or "the accuser." Greek versions of these texts transliterated the Hebrew literally as *satanas*. In many of these texts, the accuser is one who is part of God's heavenly court, such as an angelic being (Zechariah 3, Job 1:6–12; 2:1–7), but in Psalm 71:13, the term is used generically for people who accuse others.

During the two or three centuries before Jesus, the idea of a satan figure began to evolve in Judaism. A number of the Dead Sea Scrolls depict an evil figure who is an angel of darkness or a ruler of this world.[3] This figure is sometimes called Belial or Satan. So in the few hundred years between the completion of the books in the Hebrew Bible and the writing of the New Testament, understandings of Satan shift from being a title for "the accuser" (Hebrew: *hasatan*) that might be applied to any being fulfilling that role, to the name of a single evil figure that opposes God and accuses or deceives God's people.

By combining these various names—dragon, serpent, devil, Satan, deceiver—John is making an implicit theological argument that there has been one evil force opposing God throughout human history. Readers might know this evil by a variety of names or images, but John wants them to know it is all the same thing. John, however, draws on more than just names and a Hebrew Bible tradition to make his point: he also uses a well-known mythical story to bring Gentile hearers into his account of good and evil. We turn to these myths now.

Drawing on Mythology

The moment the dragon appears, it brings death and destruction in its wake. John describes seeing a vision of the dragon attacking the heavenly woman in order to destroy the child she has just given birth to (12:4). The child is "snatched away" to God's throne for protection, and the woman flees to the wilderness, where a place has been made for her (12:5–6). The drama is not over, however. Immediately, a war breaks out in heaven, and John describes a scene where the angels of

---

[3] The Dead Sea Scrolls (DSS) are a collection of texts found in caves at Qumran. They date from the third century BCE to the first century CE. They were discovered in the 1940s and have had a significant impact on what we know about ancient Judaism in the period between the Hebrew Bible and the New Testament. Some of the texts are recognizable parts of the Hebrew Bible, while others are entirely new and include liturgical texts, apocalypses, community rules, and alternative renderings of biblical texts.

the archangel Michael fight with the angels of the dragon in the sky. They defeat the dragon and cast him down to earth (12:7–9). Now on earth, the dragon continues to pursue the woman and her baby, but this time nature itself helps protect them (12:13–17). In this section of Revelation, John is drawing on a couple of mythical traditions—one from Greco-Roman mythology and one from the Jewish tradition.

The story of Python pursuing Leto was well known in antiquity, preserved in ancient literature as well as in imagery that decorated vases, temple reliefs, and the carvings around the altar to Zeus in Pergamum. In Greek mythology, Leto was a goddess who became pregnant with Zeus's children—twins named Apollo and Artemis. Zeus's wife Hera is understandably jealous, so she sends Python after Leto to destroy her and her children. Python is just what he sounds like—a serpentine monster, sometimes described as a dragon, who was thought to live near Delphi in Greece. Python pursues Leto as she searches for a safe place to give birth to her children. There are many versions of this story, but in some of them, Leto is aided by Zeus, who sends a wind that enables her to cross the seas; in others, she becomes bird-like and flies to safety. Both of these elements are preserved in Revelation 12, where the heavenly woman grows wings and flies like an eagle (12:14) and where nature helps to hide her when the earth swallows up the waters that threaten to sweep her away (12:16).

In the Greek myth, Leto does manage to give birth, and when her son Apollo grows up, he seeks out Python and kills him in revenge. The epic battle between Apollo and Python is recorded in the *Homeric Hymn to Apollo* (sixth century BCE). In Homer's version, Python is called Drakaini.

While this myth might be unfamiliar to many modern readers, Revelation's first audience would have recognized the story John was telling. These are the stories they grew up with, perhaps a bit like the fairy tales many of us were told during our childhoods. John cleverly reimagines the story, casting Leto as the heavenly woman whose off-spring (Jesus and his followers) are pursued by a great evil dragon. God, like Zeus, comes to their aid. We haven't got to the last part yet, where the son will come and avenge his mother by killing the dragon, but it's coming. The way John tells the story, we are set up to expect it.

The second myth that John draws upon is that of Satan, or Lucifer, being cast out of heaven. The dragon's attack on the woman sparks an angelic war in heaven: Michael and his angels fight the dragon and his angels, resulting in the dragon being defeated and thrown out of heaven down to earth (12:7–9).[4] It is a version of the fall of Satan, or Lucifer, which has its origins in the Jewish tradition.

Isaiah 14:12–15 describes a Day Star who is thrown down to Sheol (the realm of the dead) for trying to set up a throne for himself in order to be like God. Note that the Latin word for Day Star is *Lucifer*. Ezekiel 28:16–17 possibly alludes to a similar story in the proclamation against Tyre, describing how something that God had created and placed in Eden became arrogant and corrupted. The idea of an angelic or heavenly figure who is cast out of heaven became quite popular in the Enochic literature that predates the New Testament. The text of 1 Enoch contains several versions of fallen angel stories, including a list of the names of all the angels that have been cast out of heaven and now work with Satan (1 Enoch 21:1–10; 69:2–3; 86:1–6; 87:1–2). In many of these accounts in 1 Enoch, the angels and stars are interchangeable terms for divine beings that fall from the sky. The idea of a fallen angel persists in the New Testament era. It lies behind the line Jesus says according to Luke's Gospel: "I watched Satan fall from heaven like a flash of lightning" (Luke 10:18). Other ancient non-canonical literature also draws upon this fall of Satan myth (see 2 Enoch 29–31), and it was made popular in modernity in John Milton's 17th-century poem *Paradise Lost*.

The idea that Satan was cast out of heaven became popular precisely because it gave an explanation for the presence of evil on earth. It was a way of maintaining that God made the world and "it was very good"

---

[4] Michael was well known as an archangel, or prince, by the time the New Testament was written (see Daniel 10:13; Jude 9; 1 Enoch 9:1). The idea of named angels implies an angelic hierarchy that is part of this tradition.

(Gen 1:31) *and* that evil was present and active in the world. John doubles down on this idea in the way he concludes the vision: "When the dragon saw that he had been thrown down to earth, he pursued the woman" (Revelation 12:13). When she manages to escape, readers are told the dragon became angry and instead focussed his energy on pursuing the woman's offspring. A single son has now become many, defined as those "who keep the commandments of God and hold the testimony of Jesus" (12:17). John reshapes and combines ancient myths to tell a recognizable story of a monster pursuing a goddess to kill her divine son. This monster gets thrown out of heaven and now pursues God's children on earth.

Rhetorically, John's use of these myths does really important work to explain the suffering these Christian communities are facing. Instead of hostility and suffering being signs of God's abandonment, or even of God's impotence, they are reimagined as proof that God is winning. The heavenly battle in 12:7–12 is the first of three scenes in which God systematically defeats the dragon, each one more serious than the last. Here, the dragon's loss results in him being cast out of heaven and relegated to earth. Later, he will be bound in a pit for a thousand years (20:1–3) before finally being utterly destroyed (20:7–10). In other words, readers who are experiencing evil and suffering are being told that this is precisely because God is in control and sorting things out. It is part of the plan.

We have seen that John draws these various traditions together to make the point that this dragon is the same antagonist found in Jewish and Greek traditions—an evil figure known by a variety of names, yet always the same. One of the traits of a monster is that they can morph and appear in different forms at different times. John portrays evil as this primordial force that has always opposed God and has appeared in different guises throughout history: the ancient serpent in Eden, the mythical chaos monsters of the deep, the accuser (Hebrew: *hasatan*) that tests God's people, and the one who continues to deceive humanity. Next, we turn to John's portrayal of this evil as being manifest in the Roman Empire and its beasts.

The Beasts (13:1–18)

The Sea Beast

The scene shifts, leaving the dragon standing on the seashore. Immediately, we meet a new character: a beast, rising out of the sea (13:1). The sea is important as it evokes Daniel 7, where the four beasts rise out of the sea, representing kings and their empires.[5] From the perspective of Asia Minor, Rome is across the sea, and this is our first hint that this beast might have something to do with Rome specifically.

The symbols associated with the beast are now somewhat familiar: he has ten horns and seven heads, like the dragon, as well as ten diadems. These features suggest power and authority, much like they did on the dragon and the Lamb. Trying to figure out how ten horns and diadems are dispersed across seven heads will only hurt your brain, so don't bother. The weird math is a reminder that we are in the realm of symbolism, not literalism. The animalistic features function in a similar way—on the one hand reminding us of Daniel's four beasts (lion, bear, leopard, and ten-horned creature), and on the other hand functioning as symbols for speed, power, strength, and the traits of predators. This is not a nice beast. It is wild, powerful, and dangerous, and it has been given all the power and authority of the dragon (13:2).

Less familiar are the "blasphemous names" that cover the beast's heads (13:1). We don't know exactly what these words were, but it is likely that an ancient reader would have immediately thought of the titles that kings and emperors claimed for themselves—Lord, Savior, Benefactor, Divine, and God or Son of God. We know from ancient coinage, inscriptions, and historical accounts that Roman emperors used these titles regularly. In John's view, they are titles only God deserves, which makes them blasphemous when used by anyone else.

---

[5] The four kingdoms in Daniel are described as "four great beasts," each with their own animalistic symbolism (Daniel 7:3). They are thought to represent the empires that defeated or oppressed the Jews—Babylon, Media, Persia, and Greece.

Another surprising symbol is that one of the beast's heads has a mortal wound (13:3), a death blow that has healed up. This seems to be a source of amazement, causing people to follow the beast and worship it. In fact, both this beast and the dragon are now worshiped by "the whole earth" who follow them (13:3). You know who else in Revelation has a mortal wound? The Lamb. The one who was slaughtered but now stands, presumably healed since he is alive (5:6). The Lamb is also worshiped, but by the whole of heaven rather than the whole earth, and the Lamb shares God's throne just like the beast shares the dragon's throne. We can start to see the parallels John has set up in his text: Dragon versus God, beast versus Lamb. In each case the evil counterpart attempts to imitate and behave in ways that belong to God.

As the scene unfolds, readers are given a narrative that accounts for why evil is ruling on earth. It is an extension of the previous scene with the dragon, but now it is more specific and located in time and place. The beast is "permitted" (one assumes by God, but it's unclear) to exercise authority for forty-two months (13:5). As I mentioned in the previous chapter, this period of time also crops up in Daniel. There, the beast is described as having ten horns, and it has three and a half years to trample the earth, devour the people, act blasphemously, and make war with God's people, the "holy ones" (Daniel 7:23–26; cf. 12:7). In Daniel, this beast is a reference to the Seleucid ruler Antiochus IV Epiphanes, who desecrated the temple in Jerusalem by setting up a statue of Zeus and banning Jewish offerings for three years. This is also the same length of time that the temple in Jerusalem is trampled by the nations earlier in Revelation (11:2), suggesting John might be rewriting and updating Daniel to depict the way Roman forces desecrated and destroyed the temple in 70 CE.[6]

The perceived power of the beast is captured in the earlier question: "who is like the beast and who can fight against it?" (13:4). This

---

[6] This occurred during the Jewish–Roman war, which began with Jewish revolts around 66 CE, included Rome's complete destruction of the Jerusalem temple in 70 CE, and continued until about 74 CE

cry reflects the perspective of the powerless in the face of a powerful foreign, militarized regime that rules "over all the nations" (13:5–10). The beast's power on earth, designated by the dragon, seems unstoppable. To whom or what is John referring? Who is this sea beast?

The Identity of 666

At the end of chapter thirteen, readers are told that the beast's name is a number and that number is 666 (13:17–18). John is clear in stating that this number can be calculated, and it is also the number of a person. It is one of the few things in Revelation that *is* actually a code. Popular theories throughout time have claimed 666 refers to a number of different people including the prophet Muhammad, Saddam Hussein, Barack Obama, Bill Clinton, the pope, and Monster energy drinks (yep, it's a theory based on some dodgy use of Hebrew). But there is a more plausible explanation from John's time and place.

John refers to the ancient practice of *gematria* when he tells them the number is a name. Each letter in ancient Greek and Hebrew alphabets had a numerical value. The equivalent today would be saying that a=1, b=2, c=3, and so on. The first nine Greek and Hebrew letters represented numbers one to nine, and the next nine letters went up in multiples of ten (10, 20, 30, 40, etc.). Any remaining letters went up in multiples of one hundred (100, 200, 300, 400). In this system, anyone's name can have a numerical value.[7]

The number 666 in Greek is chi (χ), xi (ξ), sigma (ς): 600 + 60 + 6. There are obviously lots of names that could equal 666, but the prevailing theory is that this is a reference to the emperor Nero, whose title transliterated into Hebrew would be Neron Caesar (נרון קסר).[8] These letters in the Hebrew alphabet would add up as follows:

---

[7] *Gematria* is found in Greek and Hebrew sources. We know it was common in rabbinic Judaism and there are numerous examples of *gematria* in the Talmud.
[8] Biblical Hebrew was not written with vowels, so only the consonants have numerical value.

HEBREW LETTER NAME	HEBREW LETTER	VALUE
nun (N)	נ	50
resh (R)	ר	200
final nun (N)	ן	50
qoph (C)	ק	100
samekh (S)	ס	60
resh (R)	ר	200
		Total: 666

While 666 dominates our imaginations, a significant number of ancient manuscripts of Revelation 13:18 actually have 616 as the number of the beast. This variant can be explained by tallying up the numerical value of an alternate spelling of Neron Caesar that omits the final nun in Neron: Nero Caesar.

HEBREW LETTER NAME	HEBREW LETTER	VALUE
nun (N)	נ	50
resh (R)	ר	200
~~final nun (N)~~		~~50~~
qoph (C)	ק	100
samekh (S)	ס	60
resh (R)	ר	200
		Total: 616

Of course, not every Revelation scholar is convinced that 666 (or 616) is Nero, but it is probably the best theory we have and one that makes sense of other aspects of the text.

Nero ruled as emperor from 54 to 68 CE, which means he was the emperor at the start of the Roman–Jewish war, which culminated in the destruction of Jerusalem. To say he is not remembered fondly would be an understatement. Several ancient historians, notably Tacitus, Suetonius, and Dio Cassius, portray Nero as an erratic tyrant who loved to sing and perform, and who punished anyone who showed a lack of enthusiasm for his performances. He is implicated in the deaths of both his wife and his brother, and he famously blamed Christians for the fires that broke out in Rome in 64 CE, making them a public scapegoat by arresting them, crucifying them, or throwing them to the beasts as a "punishment."

Notably, legend has it that Nero took his own life by stabbing himself. There seems to have been an unusual amount of mystery around his death compared to the deaths of other emperors. Toward the end of the first century CE, rumors emerged that Nero had not actually died and that he would return with an army to retake Rome (this is known as the *Nero Redivivus* legend). John seems to be drawing on this legend in the way he describes the beast, supporting the idea that the number 666 is a reference to this particular emperor. The mortal wound that was healed suggests a stab wound that did not actually kill him. Moreover, the reference to the beast "who was and is not but is about to ascend" (17:8, 11) might also be a way of referring to the legend about Nero's return.

The Land Beast

A second beast appears in 13:11–18, rising out of the earth this time. Land and sea are traditional pairings to denote a powerful duo. Leviathan and Behemoth are monsters from the sea and land in the biblical tradition (e.g. Job 40:15–41:2). A marble relief of emperor Claudius found in Aphrodisias (Asia Minor) depicts him as larger than life-size, standing with one foot on the land and the other foot on the sea to denote power over both domains. Such images are not uncommon in antiquity, and it is possible that John has these referents in mind as he writes.

The land beast has less power, signified by the fact it only has two horns, but it still speaks like the dragon and will act as its mouthpiece.

A hierarchy of power is described in what follows. The dragon has given some of his power and authority to the sea beast, who has now given authority to this land beast who is his agent. New Testament scholar Eugene Boring famously dubbed these three "a trinity of evil."[9]

The main role of the land beast is to make people worship and follow the sea beast under threat of death (13:15). The way worship is depicted in the strange scene that follows is actually very much in keeping with other ancient descriptions of temple practices. First, there is an image. In most ancient worship, people came to offer sacrifices or bow down before images. They worshiped something they could see. The Greek for image is *eikon*, a word that denotes something crafted, like an imprint on a coin or a bust of the emperor's head. This image is animated in some way, given breath so that it appears to speak. There are many accounts of animated statues in ancient sources. Some ancient writers seem to think that spiritual powers lay behind talking statues or other miraculous signs such as statues sweating, moving, or weeping. Others are more skeptical and describe the elaborate hoaxes that were used in temples to persuade believers through tricks. Bel and the Dragon (the extra ending of Daniel in the Greek tradition) describes priests who creep into a hollow statue to eat the food offerings and make it look like the statue itself is eating (Bel and the Dragon 1–26). The Greek satirist Lucian writes mockingly of priests who inserted tubes into the mouths of statues so that they could make it "speak" oracles while hiding out of sight.[10]

The worship orchestrated by the land beast also involves signs, such as making fire come down from heaven. This is an act of deception because, in Revelation, fire is something God rains down from heaven in judgment (8:5–7; 20:9) or uses to destroy evil (14:10; 18:8; 19:20). There is a long biblical tradition that lies behind this, such as the fires

---

[9] M. Eugene Boring, *Revelation*, (Louisville: John Knox Press, 1989), 154–155.
[10] Lucian, *Alexander the False Prophet* 26.

that consume Sodom and Gomorrah (Genesis 19)[11] and Gog (Ezekiel 38–39), or the fire that prophets summon to demonstrate power (1 Kings 18:24–38; 2 Kings 1:10–12). If the beast is making fire come down from heaven, it is another way that evil is trying to imitate God and take on the role of God.

If the first beast is a depiction of the Roman emperor Nero, scholars have various theories about the identity of this second beast. Some think it refers to a benefactor or priest of the local imperial cult who actively encourages the worship of the emperor in a provincial temple. The theory that the second beast represents a benefactor would make sense in light of the reference to it setting up an image of the first beast for people to worship (13:15). Benefactors would often donate money to local temples for the purpose of commissioning or purchasing statues and images. The second beast could also represent a priest figure. As a priest, the beast supports worship rituals and performs "signs" designed to evoke wonder. Others have suggested this land beast could be an allusion to a provincial leader or administrative council who exercises the authority of Rome in Asia Minor. In many ways, these are variations on a theme. There is general agreement that both imperial worship and power are in view here, and that this is a generic way of describing anyone who promotes the imperial cult, and therefore threatens the existence of Christians. What is significant is that political power is inextricably intertwined with religious fidelity and worship. To follow Rome is to worship the beast, which is idolatry. In John's view, it is worshiping Satan.

The Mark of the Beast

Another symbol that has taken on a life well beyond the text of Revelation is the mark of the beast (13:16–17). Contemporary conspiracy theories

---

[11]Noting that contrary to many popular interpretations, the Sodom and Gomorrah story in Genesis 19 is not a condemnation of homosexuality but a story about a town so wicked and inhospitable that the men would rape and do violence to vulnerable visitors. This is why they are condemned.

claim that this mark refers to various things, including a microchip in vaccines that allows governments to track people (this is not a real thing), barcodes, tattoos, bitcoin, neural-implants, and credit card microchips used for cashless transactions. While the mark refers to something on a wrist or forehead that allows one to buy or sell (13:16), the explanation doesn't require us to imagine that a first-century author was predicting the technological advances of the twenty-first century.

Scholars have looked for an actual referent for the mark. One theory is that ancient coinage is in view here, since coins were imprinted with the head of the emperor and/or his name. The mark (Greek: *charagma*) that allows one to buy and sell could allude to the coins that transfer from hand to hand. Others have suggested that the forehead mark could reflect the tattoos on enslaved people's foreheads, which were added either as punishment or to denote ownership. Neither of these ideas fully capture the way the mark of the beast is described in 13:16–17; and like most symbols in Revelation, we should not read these seals or marks as something literal.

We have already seen that much of the beast's symbolism and activity is a parody of either the Lamb or God. Something similar is going on here. Where God "seals" the followers of Jesus, the beast requires a "mark." The seal or a mark are similar in that they both signify belonging, identity, and protection. In Revelation, the mark of the beast is a way of saying that these people belong to the beast. As I mentioned in the previous chapter, God's followers in Revelation are marked with a seal (Greek: *sphragis*) that protects them from divine judgments and identifies them as belonging to God (7:3–4; 9:4). This seal might be a reference to baptism or the practice where a cross is drawn on one's forehead with water or oil. Such a sign is about belonging to God, even if it can't actually be seen by others. There is another tradition of signs that might also be relevant here—signs or seals that protect. For example, the blood on the doorposts protects the Hebrew people during Passover (Exodus 12), and in Ezekiel, a man marks the foreheads of those who have opposed idolatry to protect them from the Lord's fury (Ezekiel 9:2–4). The seals that Christ-followers bear in Revelation protect them in a similar way from the wrath of God associated with judgment.

To describe the mark as a parody of God's seal and not an actual thing (a coin, tattoo, etc.) does not exclude the idea that Christians living under the control of "beastly" Rome experienced tension when it came to worship practices and the imperial cult. The idea that Christians have been "sealed" and therefore do not bear the beast's "mark" (to buy and sell) points to the likelihood of economic disadvantage. It might reflect the exclusion from commercial life for Christians who did not eat idol meat or participate in guilds and cult practices associated with Rome. At another level, this is a way for John to reiterate the manner in which the beast parodies the Lamb and attempts to behave like God.

An Evil Trinity

In this chapter, we have looked at three images of evil as they are portrayed in embodied form in Revelation 12–13. This "trinity" of the dragon, the sea beast, and the land beast is the way John communicates a broader theology about evil and how it becomes manifest in the world. The dragon represents primordial evil—those forces that have always existed and continue to deceive humanity and draw them away from God. The sea beast is John's interpretation of how such evil is manifest in the systems of government and military power within his own time and place. Through vivid imagery drawn from the biblical tradition and Greco-Roman mythology, John depicts a monstrous beast whose power seems overwhelming and whose local agents compel allegiance and worship under threat of death.

Through these fantastical figures, John gives us a glimpse of what it might have felt like to live as a minority religious group in occupied territory in the ancient world. Ultimately, this is not about one man (Nero), but what he represents: Rome and the Roman Empire. It is an empire that John will describe in the chapters that follow as wholly corrupt, anti-God, and bloodthirsty.

CHAPTER SIX

The Great Whore

Now that we have explored John's visions of the dragon and his beasts (12:1–13:18), which interrupted the series of sevenfold judgments issued from the heavenly throne room, we will return to where we left off at the end of chapter four (Judgment). With the conclusion of the seven bowls of plagues (16:17–21), the scene shifts. John narrates that he is called by an angel, who issues him with an invitation: "Come, I will show you the judgment of the great prostitute, the one sitting on many waters with whom the kings of the earth have been sexually immoral (Greek: *porneuo*) and the inhabitants of the earth have become drunk with the wine of her sexual immorality" (17:1–2). John is taken to a wilderness place where the scene unfolds further. In the Bible, wilderness places are dangerous places.[1]

So far in Revelation, John has described the judgment of the earth in a range of ways, with each series of seven judgments increasing in both intensity and specificity. Those being judged are the wicked, the idolaters, and those who follow the beast. In chapters 12–13,

---

[1] Jesus is tested by the devil in the wilderness (Mark 1:12); Hagar and Ishmael almost die in the wilderness (Genesis 16 and 21); Joseph is almost killed when his brothers throw him into a pit in the wilderness (Genesis 37:22); and the Israelites think they will die when they flee from Egypt to the wilderness (Exodus 14:11). Somewhat paradoxically, these wilderness stories in the Bible also affirm that God can be found in the wilderness (see Moses's experience in Exodus 3).

readers are introduced to the beasts and the dragon, symbols for the evil that has always opposed God but is now personified and located in the Roman emperor (the sea beast). Now, a new scene of judgment unfolds: specifically, the judgment of Rome and the Roman Empire. John considers the empire to be the embodiment of evil in his world. To convey that, he uses the metaphor of a prostitute, a whore.

The Mother of All Whores (17:1–18)

I really don't like to use the language of "whore" and suspect that many of you reading this will find it equally offensive. It is disrespectful to sex workers and participates in the way society at large has dehumanized and degraded women who trade sex for money. In this chapter, I will refer to this figure as a prostitute, which is a slightly more neutral term. Yet it is worth noting that "whore" captures precisely the kind of shock value John is going for in describing Rome/Babylon in this way. At a time when Rome was personified as the goddess Roma, the "great mother" Rome, John reconfigures her as a prostitute, "the mother of all prostitutes." This parody could not be more offensive. And that is the point.

The vision John describes begins with a richly dressed prostitute riding a multi-headed scarlet beast (17:3–4). Her appearance suggests she is no ordinary prostitute, for she is adorned with jewels, pearls, and gold, and her scarlet or purple clothing also indicates her wealth. In the first century, purple/scarlet dye (it's the same word in Greek: *kokkinos*) was derived from a certain insect, meaning that it was scarce and expensive due to the labor involved in its production. Only the wealthiest citizens wore scarlet (*kokkinos*).

In Rome, prostitution was legal and men fraternizing with prostitutes was tolerated. But, much like today, there was a hierarchy of prostitution. Courtesans (Greek: *hetaira*) were at the top of the pecking order and may have served as companions for royalty or elite men. John refers to the woman in Revelation 17 as a *pornē* (the Greek term for prostitute) rather than a *hetaira*, although, at first glance, she might seem to fit into this latter category given her lavish attire. John will, however, soon disrupt and complicate the image.

In addition to her clothing and jewels, this female figure is drunk with the blood of the saints. Being drunk is a behavior one might expect of a prostitute associated with ancient brothels and bars. She also seems to be tattooed with a name that doesn't describe her as an ordinary prostitute but, instead, labels her as the "mother of prostitutes and of detestable things." This name suggests her actions result in ongoing pollution through sexual immorality. The practice of tattooing a person's crimes onto their head was carried out against enslaved people; this functioned as a way to further degrade and dehumanize them by identifying them solely by their actions. A number of prostitutes in this period were enslaved women who had no agency over their own bodies, and they might similarly have been tattooed. John's metaphor has therefore shifted the reader's expectations from wealthy courtesan to enslaved prostitute. As John goes on to describe this "great prostitute," he becomes even more critical. The golden cup in her hands is "full of the abominations and impurities of her fornication" (17:4), effectively implying that she is dirty and defiled.

The beast is also scarlet, like the woman's clothing, and thus offers a slight adaptation of the fiery red dragon, which likewise has seven heads and ten horns. And, like the sea beast, this beast in Revelation 17 is covered in blasphemous names. The imagery here suggests the prostitute is being carried and held aloft by the evil described in the previous chapters.

So who is this woman? John gives us several clues to solve the so-called mystery of her identity, none of which are particularly subtle. This is a mystery he wants all readers to understand. These clues include the following:

- Her name is Babylon the great (17:5).
- She is seated on a symbolic representation of seven hills (17:9).
- She is a great city that rules over other kings (17:18).

Babylon was the name that Christian and Jewish writers used for Rome after the destruction of the Second Temple in 70 CE. This is because the Babylonian empire was the world power responsible for destroying the First Temple hundreds of years earlier (2 Kings 25:8–9). In John's time, Rome was the equivalent world power and was responsible for destroying God's people (Jews living in Jerusalem) and God's temple.

Other features also point to the woman's identity as Rome. The seven hills of Rome were widely referred to in ancient literature. The combination of terms for hills and kings evokes images of Rome as a city and the emperors who have ruled over the empire from Rome. In this sense, Rome is a stand-in for the empire itself. Depicting cities as women is typical in the biblical traditions. Tyre and Nineveh are both described as female prostitutes in the Bible because of their rebellious attitude toward God (Nahum 3:4; Isaiah 23:16–17).

Revelation 17 gets a little more complex midway through as it talks about different numbers of kings, some of whom have fallen (i.e., died) and some who will remain only a while (17:9–13). In an effort to precisely locate the time in which John is writing, scholars have attempted various ways of numbering the seven kings based on what we know about the Roman emperors. It's a fairly futile exercise and it misses the point. But there are two distinct groups of kings worth mentioning. The first are the seven kings, five of whom have fallen. These are most likely Roman emperors. I think John is being deliberately obtuse here, but he's pointing to the reality that emperors come and go; more will rise, but God will eventually put an end to them.[2]

The other group of rulers are the ten kings "who have not yet received a kingdom" but who are united in making war against the Lamb. These are likely vassal states or allies of Rome, who contribute to her power by aligning themselves with her. They are represented in the text as the dragon's ten horns. This group will eventually turn against Rome and "hate her." In what can only be described as sexualized

---

[2] The text of 4 Ezra 11–12 talks about rulers in a similar way, depicting them as wings on an eagle that rise and fall over different periods of time.

violence, John describes them stripping her naked, burning her, and rendering her desolate (17:16). Feminist scholars have highlighted that rape is implied by John's horrific imagery. The language of desolation is related to the language of desert or wilderness, and it hints at what is to come. She will become uninhabitable. A dual punishment is therefore imagined for this prostitute: rape and being rendered infertile. Both reduce her value as a woman in a patriarchal society that prizes female purity and fertility.[3]

The language throughout this scene is both violent and misogynistic. It might help (somewhat) to remember that John is describing a city and an empire which have, in his view, destroyed God's people; he is also using familiar biblical tropes to describe their downfall. Nevertheless, these texts should be read with caution. Just as problematically, John credits God with putting such desires into the hearts of the ten kings (17:17). In the Bible, God can put things into people's hearts (Exodus 35:30–34; Nehemiah 2:12) and can also harden hearts (Exodus 4:21, 7:3–22; Joshua 11:20). Here, John attributes to God the violence that these former allies now unleash upon Rome. He points to the reality that evil will ultimately turn on itself and consume its own, but he wants God to get the credit.

Rome's Crimes

In depicting Rome as a prostitute, John is using biblical prophetic imagery to point out that Rome and its empire worship a range of other gods. From John's point of view, Rome is unfaithful to God. John repeatedly refers to Babylon (Rome) as the one "with whom the kings have fornicated" (17:2; 18:3; 9). This is a paraphrase of Isaiah 23:17, where Tyre is described as a prostitute who has "prostituted herself with all the kingdoms of the earth."

---

[3] John evokes Hebrew Bible traditions when he depicts the sexualized punishment of a female-identified place. See Isaiah 47; Ezekiel 16, 23; and Hosea 1–3.

Furthermore, the harsh condemnation and imagery that John reserves for Rome is due to her association with the death of God's people. That she is drunk with the blood of the saints and of the witnesses to Jesus (17:6) indicates that she has killed God's people and, even worse, seems to have reveled in it.

As I've said earlier, we do not have evidence that Christians were systematically persecuted in the first century CE, but we do know that Emperor Nero blamed Christians for the fires in Rome and killed many of them, that the Roman army destroyed Jerusalem and leveled the Jewish temple, and that some Christians in Asia Minor suffered for their testimony and faith. John is possibly exaggerating the threat of targeted violence on Christians to make his point, and he does so by tapping into the communal memory of another empire that destroyed God's covenant people. As the new personification of Babylon, Rome too seeks to destroy what belongs to God.

The Function of John's Wonder

John describes his reaction to Rome/Babylon as one of amazement (17:6). The Greek word here (*thaumazo*) can mean wonder, marvel, or astonishment, and it can carry either a positive sense of being impressed by something or a negative sense of being distressed by the marvel one is seeing. The angel's question to John—why are you so amazed/impressed?—suggests John might be a little *too* struck by what he sees. This is consistent with the way *thaumazo* is used throughout Revelation (cf. 13:3). After all, the prostitute's rich clothing, fantastic steed, and the fact that "the kings of the earth have committed fornication with her" suggest she is seductive. John seems to be momentarily impressed.

This short scene functions rhetorically to rebuke not just John, but any reader who might be impressed by Rome's power and glory or who desires what Rome offers. It is not just that Rome might be seductive; it is also about what she represents. As Huber writes, "the image of the Whore...points to the seductive nature of assimilation."[4] To desire Rome is to desire assimilation to the dominant culture, a posture strongly condemned in the messages to the seven churches (see chapter two). To counteract such a possibility, Revelation portrays Rome not as a beautiful courtesan, queen, or goddess, but as a drunk and blood-thirsty whore who is fully aligned with evil and who will be destroyed by God.

The Fall of ~~Babylon~~ Rome (18:1–24)

Angels and angelic announcements drive much of the narrative in Revelation. The next scene opens with yet another angel, this time crying out in a mighty voice: "Fallen, fallen is Babylon the great" (18:2). This is not the first time the fall of Babylon has been announced. In 14:8 a different angel declared the same thing, and in 16:19 we heard that "God remembered Babylon and gave her the wine-cup of the fury of his wrath." Now we receive a more detailed description of the judg-ment that has already been declared, and we gain further insights into the reasons for it.

John draws upon prophetic tradition when using the language of "fallen, fallen is Babylon." In particular, he reworks two passages from Isaiah and Jeremiah.

"Look, there they come, riders, horsemen in pairs!"
"Fallen, fallen is Babylon; and all the images of her gods
lie shattered on the ground." (Isaiah 21:9)

Babylon must fall for the slain of Israel, as the slain of all the earth have fallen because of Babylon. (Jeremiah 51:49)

---

[4] Huber, "Gazing at the Whore", 316.

Isaiah frames the fall of Babylon by focusing on the shattered images of the gods. In other words, Isaiah's concern is idolatry. Jeremiah stresses Babylon's responsibility for killing Israelites. John combines both of these in the way he frames the charges against Rome. The language of fornication or sexual immorality (Greek: *porneia, porneuo*) appears numerous times through this section, but John doesn't have actual sexual practices in mind here. Rather, he continues to use sexual promiscuity as a metaphor for religious infidelity or idolatry. In addition to idolatry, Rome is responsible for the blood of the saints and witnesses, echoing Jeremiah's charge against Babylon (17:6; 18:24).

In much the same way that John portrays Rome, the prophetic texts of Isaiah and Jeremiah contain long passages that narrate the demise of Babylon (and Nineveh and Tyre), describing a vibrant city that has become the haunt of wild animals (Isaiah 13–14; Jeremiah 50–51; cf. Ezekiel 26–27; Isaiah 23). In what seems like a scene from one of those contemporary apocalypse movies, John describes Rome as becoming a wasteland. If you can imagine Will Smith's character walking through the empty streets of New York in *I am Legend*, or the wasteland that is the world in *Mad Max*, you get the picture. Streets that were once full of luxurious living are now the dwelling place of unclean animals, demonic spirits, and the burnt-out remains of buildings.

In addition to idolatry and violence, Rome is strongly critiqued for her self-glorifying arrogance in making herself a queen (18:7) and her economic inequality. She has "lived luxuriously" (18:7) and clothed herself in fine purple linen, gold, and jewels (18:16). This inequality is reinforced through the viewpoints of merchants, kings, and shipmasters who mourn and lament Rome's demise. These are the groups who profited from her economic systems. The merchants grew wealthy from the demand for luxury goods (18:3, 11–17), the kings benefited from her protection and relationship (18:3, 9), and the shipmasters and sailors grew rich as the result of trade (18:17–19). These groups weep and mourn as they watch Rome burn. It is not just goods that are destroyed and lamented. There is an ominous aside in the list of trade items that are mourned by the merchants. In addition to the exotic spices and luxury items are "sheep, horses, chariots, and bodies, the lives of humans" (18:13). Instead of the usual word for an enslaved person (*doulos*), John uses the language of "bodies" and "souls," or "lives of humans," thus painting a stark picture of the dehumanizing effects of enslavement.

Rome was a major locus of the slave trade in the ancient world, and the city's economy relied upon it. Many of the enslaved people sold in Roman marketplaces in the first century CE were captives of war. Others were children, either born into enslavement or abandoned. Others again were those arrested and imprisoned during the Jewish revolts. The Jewish historian Josephus records that "thousands" of Jewish prisoners were sold into enslavement after the Jewish revolt in 70 CE.[5] Slave traders became incredibly wealthy from these taken "bodies." So when Rome is destroyed (*albeit* in John's imagination), her slave trade will be, too.

John's depiction of Rome as a "great prostitute" who is corrupt and bloodthirsty undermined his readers' perceptions of Roma as a goddess and savior who brought peace to the region. Similarly, the laments over the fall of Babylon/Rome function to highlight the inequality of this empire, where some profited greatly while others suffered and were enslaved. The implication is that, from the perspective of John and his community, there is nothing to mourn in the downfall of Rome.

A Call to Believers to "Come Out"

While much of Revelation 18 records the lament of merchants, kings, and shipmasters to narrate the fall of Rome, there is one direct address to believers. In 18:4, a heavenly voice—this could be God or an angelic

---

[5] Josephus, Jewish War 6.418–20.

being (the text is not specific)—calls "my people" to withdraw from Babylon. Again, John is using language from Jeremiah:

> Come out of her, my people!
> Save your lives, each of you,
> from the fierce anger of the LORD! (Jeremiah 51:45)

> Come out of her, my people,
> so that you do not take part in her sins,
> and so that you do not share in her plagues. (Revelation 18:4)

This call to "come out" is one of the few direct addresses to believers in the text. It is noteworthy that the people are not called to take up arms or do violence, but rather to withdraw from Rome so that they are not caught up in the judgment of her sins and injustices. It is less clear who is being addressed in 18:6 with the second person plural "you (pl.) give to her as she has given." It could be a call to punishing angels, or an indefinite "you," perhaps addressed to the reader. However, given that Christians are encouraged to leave Rome in 18:4, it seems unlikely they are now called to pay her back or that they have the capacity to do so. In Revelation, only God has the power to fight the beast that is Rome.

In this passage, we see injustice clearly named as a major reason for Rome's judgment and the need for believers to withdraw. John uses hyperbolic language to describe her sins as being "heaped as high as heaven" (18:5). The NRSV translates the following phrase "and God has remembered her iniquities," but a better translation would be "God has remembered her injustices" (the Greek term *adikaios* is the opposite of justice, *dikaios*). It is the injustice of Rome, in terms of its institution of slavery, economic inequality, and violence against God's people, that garners God's attention. This is what they are called to withdraw from: participation in an economic system and state that is violent and oppressive, and that makes some people rich at the cost of others' bodies. We'll pick up the implications of this in the last chapter, but it is worth noting for now that this call to withdraw from corrupt and unjust systems is one of the significant contributions of Revelation's theology for the contemporary world.

Heaven Rejoices (19:1–10)

The heavenly chorus in Revelation functions a bit like the chorus in a Greek play. That is, they declare to the audience what is true or real and tell them how to feel about what they have just witnessed. Immediately following John's vision of the demise of Rome, the multitudes in heaven burst into praise, declaring God's judgments to be "true and just." They cry,

> God has judged the great prostitute who corrupted the earth with her sexual immorality and has avenged upon her the blood of his servants. (19:2)

Through the heavenly chorus, the dual charges of idolatry and violence toward God's people are reiterated. The twenty-four elders and four living creatures add their voices to the multitude of saints, and a divine voice from near the throne tells them all to "praise our God" (19:5). The scene builds as the number of voices becomes like the "sound of many waters" and "mighty thunder." What they announce next is God's solution to the great prostitute that was Rome.

A Virginal Bride to Replace a Whore

I still don't want to use "whore" language, but here it captures the starkness of the contrast John is making. If Rome is the great whore—"mother of whores"—then the newly remade Jerusalem is a virginal bride. Here, John draws on the timeless cliché of the virgin-whore binary which equates sexually "pure" women with righteousness and sexually active women with sin. Using these stereotypes of women to compare the two cities, John introduces God's replacement for Rome—new Jerusalem.

Earlier, we saw that John relies heavily on Hebrew Bible traditions of oracles against the enemies of God, such as those against Tyre, Nineveh, and Babylon (Isaiah 13–14; Jeremiah 50–51; cf. Ezekiel 26–27; Isaiah 23). Yet, unlike those Hebrew Bible oracles, John does not address Rome directly; there is no "to you, O…" refrain. Instead he assumes his readers are *viewers* of Rome, not Rome herself. In doing so, he assumes an androcentric (male-centered) gaze that heightens the elements of desire in the text.[6] Male viewers (who I suspect are John's main intended audience) are offered a stark choice: they can desire *either* the whore *or* the bride, not both.

New Jerusalem won't appear fully until 21:2, when it comes down to earth from heaven. But like many of the visions in Revelation, we get a sneak preview and a prophetic utterance about her before she arrives. John uses culturally normative ideas of a bride putting on special clothes and preparing herself for marriage when he refers to the "fine linen" that Jerusalem is given to wear (19:8). Unlike the expensive fine linen worn by the prostitute Rome, Jerusalem's garments are made from the "righteous deeds of the saints" (19:8). This bride is clothed in righteousness—a fitting outfit for the bride of Christ and a direct contrast with the unrighteous deeds of Rome (cf. 18:5).

The Lamb is the bridegroom in the wedding imagery John uses here, which draws upon the covenantal biblical metaphor of God as the husband of God's people (see Jeremiah 31:32; Isaiah 54:5; Ezekiel 16:8). This idea continues into the New Testament, where it takes on a more apocalyptic tone and is frequent in the parables of Jesus that involve bridegrooms, marriage feasts, and being ready to be a guest at the wedding (Matthew 22:1–14, 25:1–13; Mark 2:19–20; Luke 5:34). In strikingly similar imagery, Paul tells believers that he has promised

---

[6] Barbara Rossing, *The Choice Between Two Cities: Whore, Bride, and Empire in the Apocalypse* (New York: Bloomsbury Publishing, 1999), 19. Even if John's audience includes women, he assumes the male experience as normative.

them in marriage to Christ and wants to present them "as a pure virgin" (2 Corinthians 11:2). In Revelation the imagery is multi-layered. The Lamb's bride is new Jerusalem, which is a glorious and bejeweled city (21:2, 15–21). As the eternal city that is remade by God, it is a dwelling place for all God's people. Believers therefore occupy two roles at the wedding. They are invited to the eschatological wedding feast as guests, which is a blessing in and of itself (19:9), *and*, as inhabitants of new Jerusalem, they enter into a covenantal relationship with the Lamb.

Virgins, Whores, and Empires

Revelation 17:1–19:10 is, in some ways, straightforward. In a parody of ancient descriptions and images of the goddess Roma, Rome is depicted as a prostitute and her violent downfall is described in significant detail, in much the same way the Hebrew Bible's prophetic texts described the fall of Babylon and other enemies of God. However, these few chapters of Revelation are deeply problematic for the modern reader because they appear to endorse patriarchal stereotypes regarding women's sexuality and purity. John utilizes gender stereotypes of virgin and whore to offer readers a choice between God's empire and the Roman Empire. One is good and "pure" while the other is corrupt, dirty, and therefore deserving of sexualised violence by those who desire her. And for those who desire Rome because she initially appears beautiful and rich, John's vision reveals her to be a blood-thirsty whore.

The challenge for the modern reader is to appreciate that there is a legitimate critique of empire and its injustice here, but it comes wrapped in ancient cultural norms relating to women's bodies, the control of their bodies, and male-centered ideas that assume women exist for male sexual pleasure. Despite this, at the heart of the message of these chapters is a challenge to readers not to desire what looks shiny and bright (because it is not actually of God and comes at a cost to others) and to withdraw from systems of inequality and oppression, lest one becomes corrupted by them.

The social systems that create and sustain enslavement and prostitution, and the oppressive norms of patriarchy that lie behind such systems, are never critiqued by John. (That doesn't mean we can't critique them!) Indeed, John's metaphors rely upon these systems. As we move into the final chapters of Revelation, we will see a similar dynamic at play in the final judgment and creation of God's empire. God's empire will be established but, problematically and ironically, with great violence and bloodshed.

CHAPTER SEVEN

Hell, Heaven, & the End

One of my favorite episodes of *The Simpsons* includes a scene where the family is driving home from church. Marge asks the children what they learned about in Sunday school, and Bart replies, "hell." When his parents get angry with him for swearing, Bart, with his characteristic sassiness, says, "But that's what we learned about. I sure as *hell* can't tell you we learned about *hell* unless I say *hell*, can I?" His father concedes he has a point, at which point Bart starts singing, "hell, hell, hell, hell, hell, hell, hell, hell" from the back seat of the car. The scene ends with Marge delivering the fabulous line, "Bart, you're no longer in Sunday school. Don't swear!"

Hell is a dirty word in more ways than one. For some, it is a swear word. For others, it's a key Christian belief, and telling people how to be saved from hell is a theologically essential manifestation of this belief. For others still, the concept of hell seems like an awkward bit of superstition that has no place in their conception of the divine. Then there are those for whom hell represents a vengeful theology they do not know what to do with and would rather ignore.

If we think of hell at all, it is usually as an anti-heaven, a place of fiery torment where people are sent after death to be punished and made miserable. This concept of hell is not actually very biblical. It has been shaped predominately by post-biblical traditions, such as the second century CE *Apocalypse of Peter* and the late fourth century CE *Apocalypse of Paul*, as well as the depictions of hell in medieval art and in literary works such as Dante's *Inferno*. We shall see later in this chapter that the Bible itself offers little in terms of actual descriptions of hell and what happens there.[1]

One of the prevailing ideas about Revelation is that it condemns wicked people to hell. But it actually does not. In fact, I am going to say quite boldly that there is no hell in Revelation, at least not in the sense it is often understood today. Instead, we get a series of visions of the End, when evil is progressively destroyed until Death and Hades (the realm of the dead) themselves are destroyed.[2]

In Revelation, the end of human history and the radical reordering of the cosmos are depicted in seven snapshots, or short scenes. Unlike the series of judgments earlier in the book, they are not explicitly numbered, but I can't help but think John might be having a bit of fun with the number seven here. These snapshots include:

1. the divine warrior on the white horse (19:11–16);
2. the defeated armies left to die (19:17–21);
3. Satan bound for a thousand years (20:1–3);
4. the judgment of Satan (20:4–10);
5. the end of Death and Hades (20:11–15);

---

[1] In the Gospels, we do get glimpses of ideas about "hell" or the realm of the dead, but these are usually part of a rhetorical appeal to moral action rather than attempts to systematically describe an afterlife (Luke 16; Matthew 25). Visionary tours of hell tend to occur in later Christian texts such as the *Apocalypse of Peter, Apocalypse of Zephaniah*, and *Apocalypse of Paul*, although they have precursors in Greek literature (e.g. Homer's Odyssey, 11) as well as some early Jewish texts. For more information, see Martha Himmelfarb, *Tours of Hell: An Apocalyptic Form in Jewish and Christian Literature* (Minneapolis: Augsburg Fortress Press, 1985).

[2] I have capitalized Death to denote that it functions as a force in Revelation; one that Christ has conquered through his resurrection. In John's theology, even though people still die a natural death or face an end to mortal life, the permanent state of Death is no longer the fate of humanity.

6. recreation: new Heaven and new Earth (21:1–8);

7. New Jerusalem (21:9–22:5).

John's characteristic "then I saw" punctuates these scenes, moving the narrative forward and continuing to create a sense of urgency. However, readers should not assume that the events in these seven scenes are happening chronologically. There is a certain progression, but there are also times when events are replayed from a different perspective. Rather than imagining John sitting still, watching each vision play out sequentially before his eyes, we might better grasp the rhetorical effect of these scenes if we imagine John looking around at what has been revealed to him; some of the action takes place simultaneously and some of it is out of sequence. (I am not assuming John is having literal visions here, although he may have been; I'm trying to capture the effect he wants to create through his storytelling.)

The Beginning of the End

As we move into these final chapters of Revelation we see that evil will be destroyed and God's empire will be established, but, problematically and ironically, with great violence and bloodshed. It seems that John uses the very tools of the empire he critiques (military might and domination) to imagine God's empire. The beginning of the end of all things happens when Christ comes out of the heavenly realm. What follows is the defeat of all evil, including Death and Hades. Then God recreates the earth and the heavens in a scene that suggests a return to Eden, but with a twist. Let's begin with the return of Christ.

Christ as Divine Warrior (19:11–16)

When we think of the second coming (the return of Christ), I suspect the image that often comes to mind involves Jesus dressed in a flowing white robe, floating gently down to earth on a cloud. That, at least, is the Sunday school version of events I picture in my head. Meanwhile, in the text of Revelation, readers have been led to expect that Jesus will return as a bridegroom (19:7–9). But when the second coming is eventually described, it completely overturns our expectations. Instead of a gentle bridegroom, Jesus re-enters the narrative in 19:11 as a divine warrior who proceeds to annihilate his enemies. It is the war to end all wars.

The scene in 19:11–16 is dense with imagery that requires some unpacking. First, the open door to heaven functions in the opposite way to 4:1, when John was invited up to heaven to see the throne room. Now the opened door means Christ can *come out* from heaven, presumably to earth. He is followed by "the armies of heaven," dressed in white robes and riding white horses (19:14).

How do we know it is Christ who leads these armies? The figure riding the white horse is not explicitly identified as Christ in this passage, but John leaves us lots of clues as to his identity. To begin with, the rider is named "faithful and true" (19:11), echoing the names given to Christ in the opening narrative, where he was introduced as the "faithful witness" (1:5). This rider's eyes are described as being like flaming fire, and a sharp sword comes from his mouth (19:12, 15); both of these details connect him to the vision of Christ in 1:12–16, thereby giving us further evidence of his identity. Moreover, new symbols are added to the earlier iconography, which again confirm the rider is Christ: now, he wears diadems as symbols of his kingship, reminding us of the kingship claimed by the beast in 13:1 and the dragon in 12:3. And while we are told he has a mysterious name that no one but himself knows, the next verse reveals his name is "the Word of God" (19:13). A few verses later, two other names are ascribed to him, this time written on his clothing and his thigh: "King of kings and Lord of Lords" (19:16). So while the names Jesus and Christ are never used in this passage, John makes it clear that a kingly warrior Christ figure is being depicted here. While we have hints of a militarized Messiah in other New Testament texts, this is by far the most developed portrayal within the Christian canon.

The Christ-rider's white horse is also significant. Those who are saved in heaven wear white as a symbol, either of their purity or of having been washed clean and made worthy to stand before God (3:5, 18; 4:4; 6:11; 7:9–11). The armies of heaven that follow Christ also wear white linen, connecting them to the martyrs and saints who were given white robes and told to wait for a little while (6:11, 19:14). Like the Christ-rider, they too ride white horses. According to ancient historians, victorious military leaders sometimes rode white horses during their victory parades.[3] When Christ comes out on a white horse in Revelation 19, it is a bold declaration that victory is already his.

The most threatening symbol to note is that Christ's clothing is dipped or washed in blood (19:13). The Greek word here is *baptein*, which generally means "to wash" (it's the word we get "baptism" from), but when it's used to describe clothing and color, it suggests the actions of dyeing fabric. The question is, whose blood is on the robe? Is this a reference to Jesus's own blood that was shed on the cross? Does it therefore symbolize his martyrdom? Or does the blood belong to the enemies who have been slain with his sword?

It is tempting to say that this is Jesus's blood, as that makes it a slightly more palatable image. In Revelation, Jesus's blood is efficacious and can bring release from sins (1:5; 5:9) and make the robes of his followers white—a symbol of their salvation (7:14). The Lamb's blood functions as a shorthand way to refer to his death or martyrdom, and it is given as the reason believers can conquer evil (12:11). But the main support for the view that Jesus's cloak is dipped in his own blood is that Jesus has not yet killed anyone in this scene, so the blood *must* be his. Yet Revelation does not work in a linear manner. Things are declared or revealed in advance of the action and are sometimes shown far before the relevant details are narrated. I think this is the effect John wants to create here. John evokes Isaiah 63:1–3 where God is depicted as a warrior returned from battle in blood-stained robes to announce his victory over Edom. In that passage, God is

---

[3] Herodotus, *The Histories,* 7.40, 9.63; Dio Cassius, *Roman History* 43.14.

also said to "tread the wine press" in anger. This allusion to Isaiah points to the blood belonging to the enemies who have (already) been defeated by Christ. We can compare these two passages to better see the similarities.

ISAIAH 63:1–3	REVELATION 19:13–15

"Who is this that comes from Edom,
 	
    from Bozrah in **garments stained crimson?** ...
 	
"It is I, announcing vindication,
    mighty to save."
 	
**"Why are your robes red,
    and your garments like
    theirs who tread the wine
    press?"**
 	
"I have trodden the winepress alone,
    and from the people no one
    was with me;
**I trod them in my anger
    and trampled them in my
    wrath;
their juice spattered on my
garments...**
	He is clothed in **a robe dipped in blood,** and his name is called The Word of God. And the armies of heaven, wearing fine linen, white and pure, were following him on white horses. From his mouth comes a sharp sword with which to strike down the nations, and he will rule them with a rod of iron; **he will tread the winepress of the fury of the wrath of God the Almighty.**

The way John writes this scene, combined with the allusion to Isaiah 63, means that we as readers are invited to imagine this divine warrior with his flaming eyes, sword-wielding mouth, and blood splattered clothing *and* to recognize him as the victorious Christ returned from battle. It is a battle that is already won.

A Battle Won (19:17–21)

Despite expecting a war, readers are never really given one. There is no fighting or marching or charging into battle. Rather, an angel calls the birds of the air to a feast, a "great supper of God" (19:17). The food they are offered at this feast comprises the corpses of the defeated armies. To highlight the breadth of the defeat, different groups within these vanquished armies are named: the birds eat the flesh of kings, captains, horses and their riders, the free and the enslaved, the mighty and the small (19:18). These are the same groups mentioned earlier in the first series of judgments (6:15–17). By listing them again, John reinforces that *no one* can escape God's wrath.

John draws upon Ezekiel 39 to depict this gory feast. In a narrative about the defeat of Gog and Magog, birds and wild animals are called to a "sacrificial feast" that God has prepared. The feast is actually the flesh of the fallen soldiers. "You shall be filled at my table with horses and charioteers," says God, "with warriors and all kinds of soldiers" (Ezekiel 39:20). What is going on here?

These biblical scenes in Ezekiel 39 and Revelation 19 tap into the fear of not being afforded a proper burial. In Jewish tradition, as in most societies, giving proper care to a dead body was important. Along with cleaning rituals, prayers, and mourning, this care included burial in a grave. Burial functioned to keep the deceased in their ancestral homelands, as well as marking their resting place. It was a way to keep connection and identity with both kin and the land, even after death. To leave a body uncovered in a foreign place, where it might be eaten by wild animals, was a form of punishment or a "double death."[4] It meant there was no return to the family lands, no burial, and no marked grave. A person's identity was thus effectively eradicated in death, and their body was disrespected by effectively becoming food

[4] Francesca Stavrakopoulou, "Gog's Grave and the Use and Abuse of Corpses in Ezekiel 39:11–20," *Journal of Biblical Literature* 129, no. 1 (2010): 67–84 (see especially pp. 69–71).

for animals. John vividly portrays a frightful death as a warning to readers that they do not want to face a similar fate. This use of fear to motivate readers to remain faithful to Christ is a standard type of rhetoric at this time.

The next scene (Revelation 19:19–21) backtracks to the armies of the beast, which are gathering against Christ and his heavenly army. Without pause, readers are simply told that Christ captured the beasts and the false prophet and threw them into the lake of fire (more on that below). All the followers of the beast are killed with the mouth-sword of the warrior Christ, rather than being thrown into the lake of fire.

The stark contrast between Christ and the beast (and their respective armies) presents readers with two choices or paths. Following Christ leads to victory. Following the beast leads to death, and not just any death but a violent and shameful double death, where one's corpse will be picked clean. The scene ends on an ominous note: John reports that all the birds invited to feast on the fallen "were filled/satiated with their [victims'] flesh" (19:21).

The End of Death and Evil (20:1–15)

The scene shifts from this grotesque feast to a depiction of the dragon being bound by an angel. This angel somehow manages to seize the dragon and throw him into a bottomless pit, where he must remain for one thousand years (20:1–3). Here, John reuses the four names for the dragon we encountered in Revelation 12:9: he is the dragon, that ancient serpent, the devil, and Satan. Several questions emerge, not all of which are answerable. If an angel can bind Satan like this, why hasn't it happened earlier? Where is this pit? And, why is Satan to be held there for only a thousand years? We'll focus on this last question, as it forms the basis for all sorts of ideas—some reasonable and some rather weird—about what happens at the End when Christ returns.

The Millennium (20:1–6)

The idea of a millennium—a one-thousand-year period when Christians will reign in peace—looms large in the Christian imagination. Complex theories about the timing and nature of this millennium have developed out of these few verses at the beginning of Revelation 20 (with the addition of other bits of the New Testament). Here are the three most common approaches to understanding the millennium:

1. **Amillennialists** believe the thousand years does not denote a literal period of time before Christ's second coming; rather, it refers symbolically to the time between the two comings of Christ. This, they believe, is the time in which Christians are currently living.

2. **Postmillennialists** believe the thousand years is a literal period of time, during which the gospel is preached freely because Satan remains bound in the pit. The millennium therefore provides the opportunity for more people to be saved and for the gospel to be preached to the ends of the earth. Christ will return after this thousand-year period comes to an end.

3. **Premillennialists** believe Christ's second coming occurs before the thousand-year period begins, but this one gets complicated and has various versions. Here are the two main ones:

   a. Christ comes to earth and, after a "battle" (time of conflict), establishes his kingdom here. This kingdom is sometimes thought of as a kind of theocracy, where Christians rule the world with Jesus.

   b. There will be a rapture and a resurrection of the dead to reign with Christ during the thousand-year period. In some versions of this premillennial view (such as those held by Adventists), believers are raptured up to heaven, where they reign with Christ. The "pit" in which the dragon is bound is actually located on earth, so people left behind (yes, pun intended!) on earth face a time of suffering because of rampant evil.[5]

What does the text of Revelation say about the millennium? I'm personally not convinced that any of these views capture the dynamics of Revelation well, but let's deal with the last and most popular theory first, which assumes a rapture and an earth left in disarray. This theory matches the text of Revelation least well. First of all, while Revelation reveals that those who have already died in Christ are alive in the heavenly realm, at no time is there a mass beaming up of Christians to meet Christ in heaven. Christians who attempt to read Revelation literally have to do some creative cut-and-paste proof-texting from other parts of the Bible to insert a rapture into Revelation 19–20. The text often used as evidence of a "rapture" is 1 Thessalonians 4:17, although I would argue this does not refer to a rapture either.[6] Contrary to any notion of a rapture, Christ comes out of heaven to meet the armies of the dragon in an unspecified place, possibly earth. The movement described in Revelation is of God toward humanity, not humanity toward God.

Second, nowhere else in Revelation is the earth referred to as a pit (literally *abyss* in Greek). This is language for a place under the earth, and it refers to an ancient worldview where the earth is flat, heaven is above, and the realm of the dead is below. The point of binding Satan in an abyss in Revelation is that "he cannot deceive the nations" (20:3). It is a way of suggesting God has limited the power of Satan. The amillennialist view reflects this aspect best with its view that God

---

[5] Note that the idea of a rapture of the faithful prior to a period of tribulation began in the 19th century and represents a late addition to the tradition.

[6] 1 Thessalonians 4:17 reads: "Then we who are alive, who are left, will be caught up in the clouds together with them to meet the Lord in the air, and so we will be with the Lord forever" (NRSV). The imagery used by Paul here is typical of royal processions: it imagines a scene where people meet the coming emperor or king outside the city gates to escort them into the town.

has already limited the power of Satan in the death and resurrection of Christ; yet Christians live in an in-between time waiting for the full defeat of evil at the End.

Paralleling the binding of Satan for the figurative thousand years (20:2) is the reign of saints with God for the same length of time. What readers are shown in 20:4–6 is the first resurrection, which involves a group who co-reign with God. These two millennial periods are not necessarily the same thousand years (something the theories above assume), although they could be—John is not clear. But we have already met this group of saints at various points throughout Revelation, suggesting their reign in heaven has already begun (1:5–6; 6:9–11; 7:13–15; 17:14). These are the people who have died without worshiping the beast (20:4), and while not everyone is a martyr, there is a clear reference to martyrs within this group when John refers to those who "had been beheaded for their witness" (20:4). They now reign with Christ and are given thrones to help judge the world. This is a fulfillment of what was promised in the messages to Sardis and Laodicea (3:5, 21), as well as in the opening statement of Revelation that claims Jesus has made believers "a kingdom" (1:6).

The location of those thousand saints reigning with Christ remains vague. What is important is the "with Christ" part. They are aligned with God, rather than with the beast, and so have been rewarded. This serves as a reminder to early readers that their suffering will be rewarded and rectified. Unlike other people, it seems as though they do not have to face judgment or risk a final and second death (more on this later); instead, they have been fast-tracked to co-rule with God.

Both the end of evil and the resurrection of believers happens in stages in Revelation. There is a tension between the urgency with which John writes and the drawn-out nature of these final scenes. When the thousand years of Satan's binding are up, he is released for a short period, where he again roams the earth and deceives people (20:7–8). He musters an army that, this time, is defeated by fire from the sky (20:9). Earlier, the beast and false prophet were thrown into the lake of fire (19:20) and now Satan is, too (20:10). In the only reference to eternal torture in the book, we are told that these three figures of personified evil are "tormented day and night" in the lake of fire and sulfur. But note, humans are not included here; this is a special punishment reserved for non-human actors.

A lake of fire is a vivid image, and it's not found anywhere else in the biblical tradition or Greco-Roman literature. As an unfamiliar image, it would have stood out to ancient readers as something new, adding to its menace. One theory is that it has roots in Egyptian mythology, where a lake of fire in the underworld is associated with a second death—a final death—from which there is no return or hope of resurrection. This is the sense in which it is used for a different group to which we now turn.

Judgment Day (20:11–13)

In the scene that begins in Revelation 20:11, judgment day is described as coming in the form of a throne and a book. In some ways, this is a return to the original throne vision in Revelation 4 and its courtroom imagery. God's throne is the central image, and this time it is depicted as being white (20:11). God is not described, except as "the one seated upon" this throne and the one whose presence is so terrifying that "earth and heaven fled from God's presence." This is a theme we have already encountered in Revelation, both through images of mountains or islands disappearing when confronted with God's wrath (6:14; 16:20) and also via the idea that there is "no place" to hide from divine judgment (6:15–17; 20:11–13).

But what about the book that is opened in 20:12? In Greek, the word translated as scroll or book is the same—*biblion*. So when we read that a "book of life" is opened, it evokes the earlier scroll (*biblion*) that was sealed (20:12; cf. 5:1).[7] Readers should be on the alert. The last time we had a scene with God seated on a throne and a book being

---

[7] It also evokes the scene in 1 Enoch 90, which likewise features a throne, books being opened, and an abyss full of fire.

opened, the four horsemen of the apocalypse were unleashed, along with all the chaos that followed thereafter. This time, though, the judgment is not for those living on the earth; rather, it is for everyone who has already died. This group is presented before the throne and judged.

I want to be honest about the potentially problematic theology here. If we read Revelation 20:11–13 as a literal description of human judgment and then use it as the sole basis for a theology of salvation, we end up with a "theology of works," where everyone's deeds are listed in books and then used to determine their fate. Like any passage in the Bible, we need to put this alongside other Scriptures before assuming it supports a theology that judges people solely on their deeds over and against a concept of salvation by grace (works vs. faith is the classic distinction between these two). We might note that John is vague about what constitutes "works." This word (Greek: *erga*) can mean deeds, actions, activities, or an occupation. In whatever sense John is using the word, he doesn't offer specific examples of good or bad *erga* (works/actions). We might also note that, until this point in Revelation, the single thing determining whether one is on God's team (or not) is faith and allegiance to God. It is *who* one worships that's important. And worship is a "work"—it is a tangible action that the world can see. Lastly, we might note what is absent from John's judgment yet all too present in modern Christianity: people in Revelation are not judged on correct doctrine or correct belief. If they follow Jesus and worship God, their names are in the book of life. Precisely what they think about any particular doctrine is not a concern for this author.

The scene ends with humans whose names were not in the book of life being thrown into the lake of fire, which we are explicitly told is "the second death" (20:14). While this seems harsh, I want to stress that these people are not sent to hell. There is no concept of hell here. The only alternative to eternal life is eternal death.

Death and Hades (20:13–15)

You may have noticed that Death and Hades have capital letters in some Bibles (e.g. the NRSV, ESV, and in what I've written above). This is an editorial choice made by modern translators to indicate they are personified; that is, they act as characters in the story John tells. In the judgment scene (mentioned earlier), Death and Hades "give up their dead" to the throne. Then they face their own fate (20:13–14).

When Death and Hades are thrown into the lake of fire (20:14), it symbolizes their end and the end of all they represent. Remember, there is no coming back from the second death that is the lake of fire. There are echoes of Pauline theology here in the idea that Death itself is defeated. Paul puts it like this: "The last enemy to be destroyed is death" (1 Corinthians 15:26). Indeed, if you read 1 Corinthians 15, you'll notice several resonances with the events in Revelation 19–20. Paul and John share an understanding that salvation is available because Christ has been raised from the dead and Death itself has been defeated.[8]

Hell (A Side Note)

The Bible contains several words that end up being loosely translated as "hell" or equated with some concept of hell in popular thought. In the Hebrew Bible, Sheol is the most common word for the place people go after death. Sheol is simply the realm of the dead and everyone goes there, whether they are good or bad, Jew or Gentile. Any association between punishment and an eternal destination after death had not yet developed.

---

[8] Paul, like John, uses language of "first-fruits" for those raised from the dead (1 Corinthians 15:20, cf. Revelation 1:5, 14:4). Both authors also locate the power of Jesus to forgive sins in his resurrection and subsequent reign with God (Compare 1 Corinthians 15:17–18, 24–26 and Revelation 1:5, 11:15–17). It is this dual action of resurrection and reign that means Death and evil are defeated.

In the New Testament, there are several terms that refer to a place for the dead or a place associated with punishment. The term Hades, which is the preferred term in Revelation, comes from Greek culture, where it likewise refers to the resting place for the dead.[9] Depending what Greek literature you read, Hades is under the world, across a river at the end of the world, or in some other murky location. The idea of an immortal soul also comes from the Greek tradition, so Hades is the place where souls go. In 1 Enoch 22,[10] ideas about Hades and Sheol merge in an image of a dark place filled with pits where the souls of the dead wait for final judgment.[11]

Other Greek words sometimes translated as hell in the New Testament include Gehenna, Tartarus, or the Abyss. Of these, Gehenna is the closest to some later notions of hell as a fiery place of torment. This is because of its connection with fire and wickedness. Gehenna in the Hebrew Bible is associated with a valley where children were sacrificed, using fire, to gods like Baal (Jeremiah 7:31; 19:4–6). Drawing on this tradition, New Testament authors use it as a synonym for a place of extreme wickedness, horror, fire, and death. This term is frequently translated "hell" in the Gospels, even when it doesn't necessarily refer to something eternal that lies beyond death (see Matthew 5:22, 29; 23:15; Mark 9:43–47; Luke 12:5). We might think of it as more of a "hell on earth."

---

[9] In Greek thought, Hades was originally the god who had dominion over the dead. The god's name became synonymous with the place.

[10] This section of 1 Enoch probably dates to the 3rd century BCE. It is a Jewish text in which we can see the influence of Greek thought on Jewish religion.

[11] There is a key difference between Greek and Jewish literature when it comes to assumptions about bodies and souls and therefore what part of a human goes into the afterlife. Ancient Jewish texts do not speak of an immortal, separable soul, only a spirit-body being. The idea of a separate immortal soul that lives on even after the body has died is based in Greek philosophy. Revelation does not talk about souls, despite being heavily influenced by Hellenism; rather, it reflects a more traditional Jewish understanding of human beings as embodied spirits. When the dead are raised to face judgment, they are raised as whole people, not disembodied souls.

We will return to some of these issues later in terms of their implications for the portrayal of salvation in Revelation. What is clear, however, is that Revelation does not describe a place of eternal punishment for human beings. If you want to find evidence for hell as a place of eternal punishment for the wicked, you need to look beyond the New Testament to later literature and art.

The End: Heaven... or Something Like It

Just as there is no hell in Revelation, there is also no heaven. At least not in the sense of a place removed from the earth, up in the clouds, or on some other spiritual plane. That doesn't mean Revelation has no concept of eternal life with God. It does. But it looks like a multicultural urban garden-city, and it's right here on earth.

New Jerusalem (21:1–22:7)

When God has destroyed all evil through the second death and even terminated Death itself, the ground is laid for the arrival of something new. In the scene in 20:11–12, where God's throne is placed ready for judgment, readers hear that "earth and heaven fled from God's presence." What comes next is a new heaven and a new earth (21:1).

New things are good in Revelation's narrative. Saints sing *new* songs, the faithful are given a *new* name, and the "one seated on the throne" promises to make all things *new* (21:5). In fact, this promise to make things new is one of the few times God speaks directly in the text (cf. 1:8). New is good. It is a gift from God and a symbol of God's ongoing creative activity. In Revelation's theology, God did not just create once; God continues to create and will ultimately re-create in what is a return to Eden—but with a twist.

What appears as the new heaven and earth is the holy city of Jerusalem. This is John's answer to the Whore of Babylon (Rome). Jerusalem is the bride who was anticipated in the heavenly song of 19:7, but she now appears fully in 21:9–21. Her arrival is announced by an angel, and then John takes over as narrator of the vision. Evoking prophetic imagery, he describes himself again as "in the spirit" and is taken to a high mountain (21:10). Mountains are, of course, places of prophetic revelation in the Bible. Moses received the commandments and was given the plans for the tabernacle while he was on Mount Sinai (Exodus 24). Ezekiel is taken to a mountain to see his vision of the new temple (Ezekiel 40:2ff). Mount Zion, in particular, is thought of as God's dwelling place—the mountain to which all the nations would stream, and from where restoration (and judgment) would come at the end (Isaiah 2:3; 4:3–6; 33:5–6; Psalm 2:6; 53:6; 76:2; 102:16; 132:13).[12]

The description of New Jerusalem is dense with imagery, drawing upon and expanding similar visions in Ezekiel 40–48, Isaiah 65, and 1 Enoch 90. The city is covered in rare jewels, all the gates are pearls, the layout is a perfectly proportioned square, and the streets are pure gold (21:11–21). In other words, this is the most amazingly beautiful and dazzling city a reader could imagine—she even outshines the grandeur of Rome. She is also surrounded by a high wall that has twelve gates, each of which is guarded by an angel (21:12). While walled cities are perhaps strange to the modern reader, in antiquity, they made a city safe.

Jerusalem is the ideal city, even having a water source that runs through the middle (22:1–2). John is not the only New Testament author to imagine God's final dwelling place as a holy city (see Galatians 4:26; Hebrews 11:10; 12:22; 13:14), but his vision of this city is by far the most detailed.

Further symbolism is built into the description of Jerusalem's twelve gates and twelve foundations. Like the earlier reference to 144,000 people, John draws together the twelve tribes of Israel with the twelve apostles: the twelve tribes of Israel are the names on the

---

[12] The idea that God dwells in Zion is everywhere in the Psalms. I've only noted a few references for the sake of brevity.

gates (21:12), and the twelve apostles are the city's foundation (21:14). Christians do not replace Israel in this text; rather, they are dependent upon it and inextricably linked with it.

While there is no temple in this new city, the city itself resonates with temple and priestly imagery. The jewels mentioned—jasper, sapphire, emerald, carnelian, topaz, and a whole bunch of gems you've never heard of—are all related to the vestments of the high priest (Exodus 28) or the garden of Eden as depicted in Ezekiel 28:13. John weaves together traditions of jewel-encrusted bridal outfits, priestly garments, and even Eden itself to portray the bridal, holy, recreated, city in which God will dwell.

A skeptical reader might notice that there is a certain irony here: Rome was judged for her luxurious items, but when it comes to Jerusalem, a different standard seems to apply. Rome's problem, however, is not her wealth *per se*, but its significance. God's dwelling place deserves every decoration, because all the ornate jewels point to God's glory and power. When other cities and empires try to emulate it, they are being idolatrous in giving themselves things that rightly belong to God.

One important symbol in New Jerusalem is the Tree of Life. It is one of the strongest connections between this text and the garden of Eden in Genesis 2–3. The Tree of Life sits on each side of the river (22:2). The name (Greek: *xulon zōēs*) is grammatically singular, so it is only one tree, but somehow it straddles both sides of the river. This tree has twelve kinds of fruit, which it produces monthly. In other words, this is not like any normal tree. It is supernaturally productive. It also has supernatural leaves that are "for the healing of the nations" (22:2). A tree that brings healing and provides a life-giving source of food suggests that people are not instantly perfected when they enter New Jerusalem; rather, in this cosmopolitan city to which the nations stream, ongoing healing is needed for people to reconcile. The image reflects an understanding of God as constantly re-creating and reconciling.

Lastly, it is worth noting that the water sources are significant in this city, both in terms of what is present and what is not. Readers are told there is no sea in the recreated heaven and earth (21:1). This is a stark departure from a Genesis view of creation, where the world is divided into land, sea, and heaven. What's the significance of this? Well, the sea represents chaos and death in many biblical texts. This is why Gospel accounts of Jesus walking on water or calming the storm are in fact depicting apocalyptic events that demonstrate his identity and power over demonic and chaotic forces. In Revelation specifically, the sea is the source of the monstrous beast. Rome, or the whore, also sits on "many waters," once again associating evil with the sea (17:1). While there is to be no sea in New Jerusalem, there is the promise of a "spring of the water of life" (21:6), which becomes the "river of the water of life" that flows from the throne itself (22:1). Life is again emphasized. If the lake of fire represented the second death and total annihilation, New Jerusalem represents a second life, an abundant life.

God Comes to Humanity

John is clearly using material from 1 Enoch 90 in his depiction of the End. In the Enoch version, New Jerusalem emerges via a transformation of old Jerusalem. The metaphor in 1 Enoch points to something like a renovation. John changes his source significantly when he describes seeing New Jerusalem "come down out of heaven" (21:2). It arrives perfectly intact in all its glory as it moves from the heavenly realm to earth. In a pattern that parallels the incarnation of Jesus, God moves to be with humans at the end. The arrival of New Jerusalem is announced by a loud voice which says,

> See, the home (tent) of God is among mortals, God will pitch his tent with them as their God, they will be God's peoples and God will be with them. And God will wipe every tear from their eyes. And death will be no more, nor mourning, nor crying, nor pain will be anymore; for the first things have passed away. (21:3–4)

The word translated as "home" here is *skēnē* in Greek (and the related verb is *skēnoō*). It is the word for tent or tabernacle. We get the same verb in John 1:14: "And the Word became flesh and dwelt (pitched his tent) among us." While I'm being a bit literal in my translation here, I think the idea of God pitching God's tent among the people captures the imagination more than "dwelt." It is tangible, practical, and evocative. Imagine a God who wants to pitch their tent and camp with us!

Tent imagery also evokes the Hebrew Bible, where *skēnē* is the term used for tabernacle in the Greek translation. The tabernacle was the tent in the wilderness where God was believed to dwell, and it was where the ark of the covenant was kept (Exodus 25:1–16). As the people crossed the desert on their way to the promised land, they brought the tabernacle with them and pitched it wherever they stopped as a sign that God was in their midst. (The tabernacle was later replaced with the temple, which was also thought of as the dwelling place of God.) John inverts this tradition by showing *God* pitching a tent among the people. This is a radical affirmation of God's desire to move toward all of humanity by coming from heaven to earth in order to live among them.

Meeting God

Eugene Boring writes that, ultimately, "at the End we meet not an event but a Person."[13] We meet God. The one who has only been described vaguely by John as "seated on the throne" is now fully present in New Jerusalem, and readers are promised "they will see God's face" (22:4). Earlier in Revelation, God's face has been associated with blinding light and wrath (1:16; 6:16); now it is a source of blessing, much like in Psalm 67:1 or Numbers 6:26, where God's countenance is a source of peace.

Related to the idea of meeting God face to face is the absence of a temple in the perfected Jerusalem. John changes Hebrew Bible tradition

---

[13] Boring, *Revelation*, 215.

here, which expected a temple in a glorified Jerusalem (Ezekiel 40–48; Zechariah 14; 1 Enoch 91). In John's theology, however, the temple was only ever needed as a temporary dwelling place for God on earth and to house the sacrificial system. It was a way for God's presence to be with God's people and for people to approach God. But now that a full relationship is restored (through Jesus Christ) and people can approach God directly, John considers a temple to be obsolete.

But John goes a step further when, unusually, he calls *God* the temple, writing "I saw no temple in Jerusalem for the Lord God the Almighty and the Lamb is her temple" (21:22). There are some similarities here with John's Gospel, where Jesus refers to his body as the temple that will be destroyed (John 2:19–21). The effect is to close any gap between God and the people. No longer is there any need for rituals to cleanse oneself before approaching the divine to offer worship and sacrifices. God has made people clean, and so people have unmediated access to worship God.

Several other metaphors are used to describe the relationship between God and the people at the End. One is that of parent and child (21:7), another depicts God as the light, or sun, for the community (22:5, cf. 1:16), and another uses the image of master and servant, where God's people are tattooed on their foreheads to mark them as belonging to God (22:4). Revelation is demanding for readers, as somehow we have to hold these diverse images together. John affirms the dazzling glory of the enthroned God, yet introduces a tender intimacy in the idea that God will wipe the tears away from a person's face (21:4). Whatever image dominates or resonates most, the emphasis is that, at the End, humanity is invited to meet God face to face (22:4).

Who Is Saved? (Open Gates)

In the winding, zigzagging timeline that shapes Revelation's narrative, it can be hard to know the order of events. Even at "the End" when New Jerusalem is described and her arrival declared, there continue to be references to those outside the gates and those who are still coming in.

Three times during the description of New Jerusalem, John includes an aside about who is not in the city. The first is a list of all the people who will go to second death (21:8). This list, with a little variation, occurs three times in Revelation and reflects a fairly standard list of vices or bad behaviors (9:20–21; 22:15). Yet, when it appears again in 22:15, the group are not dead but are sitting outside the gates of the city. Similarly, those deemed unclean and those not in "the Lamb's book of life" are also outside (21:27). That then raises the question: if all the wicked people were subjected to the second death in the lake of fire at the end of chapter 20, why are some folk still sitting outside Jerusalem?

At first glance, it might seem that those who are still outside Jerusalem have to watch from the sidelines. Complicating how we might interpret this vision is the reference to the gates of the city always being open (21:25). Is this an invitation? Does it suggest there is a chance of later repentance? Some scholars think so. John seems to leave open the possibility that the wicked can still repent and enter the gates at some future date *if* they wash their robes—a metaphor for following the Lamb. He writes, "Blessed are those who are washing their robes, so that they will have the right to the Tree of Life and may enter the city by the gates" (22:14).

The other way to read this verse is as a direct call to the reader. John uses a present tense participle for "washing" (*plunō*) to suggest an ongoing action. Readers already in the process of washing their robes in the Lamb's blood (i.e. those who are prepared to suffer for and with Christ) are reminded that life in the eternal city awaits.

Blessings, Curses, and an Epilogue (22:8–21)

When John finishes describing his vision of New Jerusalem, he recounts one more story. This time, it's about himself and his reaction to all he has seen. He writes, "and I, John, the one hearing and seeing these things, when I heard and saw them, I fell down prostrate to worship at the feet of the angel who was showing them to me" (22:8). It is a rather astonishing admission for an author who has been so strong in his criticism of the idolatry of others. John worships an angel!

The scene, however, functions as an illustration of what *not* to do. John is strongly rebuked by the angel who describes themself as a fellow servant with John before commanding him to "worship God!" (22:9) This scene has played out before (19:10), suggesting angel worship was a matter of some concern in John's community. He wants to reiterate that only God (not an angel, or a prophet) is worthy of worship and therefore 22:8–9 reinforces a central message of the book.

The last few verses of Revelation are a strange mix of blessings, curses, threats, and invitations. God's eternal nature is re-stated in the alpha and omega saying of 22:13, before a wider invitation is issued from the Spirit and the bride (the city) to "come" (22:17). John also doubles down on his own authority—he warns anyone who edits his prophecy, by adding or omitting parts, will receive "the plagues described in this book" or be omitted from the Lamb's book of life (22:18–19).

One theme comes full circle and that is the testimony of Jesus. Revelation opens by declaring that the apocalypse, or revelation, is made known through the testimony of Jesus, a testimony to which John himself testifies or witnesses (1:2). Furthermore, we noted that Jesus is described as the faithful witness or testifier (1:5; 3:14), and many of the faithful are described in a similar way as witnesses (martyrs) for Jesus (2:13; 11:3; 17:6). At the end, this aspect of Christ is underscored, as the book closes with the words, "the one who testifies to these things says: 'Yes, I am coming soon'"(22:20).

John responds, "Amen. Come Lord Jesus" (22:20). At the end of his apocalypse, John invites both the readers to come to Jesus and Jesus to come to earth.

So What?

What do we do with this final book of the Bible? One of the reasons I keep returning to Revelation in my scholarly work is that I don't feel I have solved all its mysteries yet. I also know I never will, and part of me likes the fact that there will always be an element of mystery. This is not a book we can decode to uncover a definitive interpretation. Anyone who attempts to do this risks ending up in dangerous places, trying to predict the date of the End, pointing fingers at whomever they think is 666, or embracing any number of other conspiracy theories that distract us from the wisdom of this text.

There is wisdom to be found in Revelation. I leave you, my reader, with the things that continue to challenge me and my theology as a disciple of Jesus who reads Revelation regularly. I hope these things might also challenge other readers, be they of another faith or none, who read this biblical book and want to think more deeply about ethics, justice, hope, and our relationship with the whole creation.

1. Jesus Looks Different

The Jesus we meet in Revelation is pretty different to the Jesus we meet in the Gospels. For Christians who want a Jesus who is a friend, a wise teacher, or a compassionate healer, the Jesus portrayed in the Gospels is easier.[1] In Revelation, Jesus is revealed as a slaughtered Lamb-Ram,

---

[1] Jesus is also depicted as a judge in the Gospels—something that is often overlooked (see Matthew 25:31–46; John 5:22–24).

a lion, a horse-riding warrior, a bridegroom, a morning star, an angel-like shining man, and a plethora of other non-human images. This disrupts nice-guy Jesus. It challenges any attempt to domesticate Jesus as a "friend."

Our understanding of Jesus in Revelation is challenged by John's unusual symbolic representations of him. We are asked to hold together the idea that Jesus is simultaneously a martyr murdered by the Roman Empire and a military powerhouse who will slaughter all enemies in a single moment. Can we add these images to our own understandings of Jesus and what is the impact when we do?

2. Evil Is Manifest in Systems, Not People

Evil in Revelation is personified in the dragon and the two other beasts we've met. These are, of course, fantastical creatures and not actual beings. But that doesn't mean evil is not real. In John's time, evil was manifest in something very real—the Roman Empire. The way he describes the empire gives us a way to think about contemporary issues that likewise oppress, dehumanize, or do violence: the power and greed of certain corporations, the military industrial complex, States that behave like unjust empires and privilege some lives over others, mass incarceration, mandatory detention for refugees, and any system that privileges a few at the cost of many (yep, I'm looking at you, neoliberal capitalism, patriarchy, colonialism, and racism).

In a sermon preached just after the Second World War, a theologian named Tom Torrance said, "It is one of the deep hypnotic mysteries of history, that evil can become incarnate in apparently Christian form."[2] Torrance's sermon was based on Revelation, and he was making a connection between the beast's imitation of the Lamb in this text and the fact that, to many German Christians, Nazism appeared good for the

---

[2] Thomas F. Torrance, *The Apocalypse Today* (Cambridge: James Clarke & Co, 1961), 102.

community. Sometimes we cannot recognize evil for what it is because it comes wrapped in a package that looks and sounds reasonable or attractive. In Revelation, humans are not evil, but they can participate in evil and become complicit in its injustices, sometimes unwittingly.

For me, Revelation's presentation of evil as something that becomes manifest in systems challenges me to think ethically about daily choices, such as where I buy my food (am I supporting industrial farming companies that are killing the earth and ruining local farmers' lives?), where I buy clothes (are they reliant on child labor?), or how my power is sourced (is it green energy, or is it contributing to the destruction of the planet?). Revelation also challenges me to keep reflecting on how I might have internalized the racism and sexism of wider society and how to actively work against both. And, as someone who lives in Australia, it challenges me to reflect on the ways I have benefited from colonialism and consider how I might listen to, learn from, and stand in solidarity with the First Nations peoples of this land. If all this sounds a bit exhausting, yes, it can be. But I hear the call to "come out of her, my people" (18:4) as one that continues to resound and to challenge me not to participate (even when it's of personal benefit) in any system that oppresses others.

3. God Moves to this Earth

Research shows that evangelical Christians are far less likely to care about climate change than about personal or moral sins. Many Christians who hold apocalyptic worldviews seem to assume that because the whole world is going to be wiped out anyway (and Christians will go to "heaven"), it doesn't really matter what we do to the earth. I think Revelation challenges this view.

While the earth is destroyed in multiple and creative ways in Revelation, these are caused by the judgments of God, rather than by human actions. There is no mandate here for human destruction of the earth. Furthermore, at the end, John reveals a God who moves out of heaven and toward the earth to dwell with humanity. Yes, God recreates and heals the earth, but that is not an excuse for disregarding its value. On the contrary, I think Revelation challenges any notion of human escape from this earth (no beaming up to heaven) and, instead, radically affirms God's desire to be with people here on earth. It is a return to the ideal of Eden, where God walked and talked with creation.

4. Hope in the Future Changes the Present

The last key takeaway from Revelation, at least for me, is that visions of hope shape the present. John's visions are designed to motivate his readers to witness, worship, and wait with faith for the fullness of God's reign to come. They are not about predicting the future or being able to identify dates. Through vivid visions, scary scenes, and cathartic catastrophes, John persuades his readers that to be followers of the Lamb means allegiance to God alone, even when this comes with personal cost. The promise that God will make everything right in the end empowers followers of the Lamb to live with courage and hope in their present time. The hope offered in Revelation is the hope that a victim will become a victor and that justice will replace injustice.

Visions of hope shape the present, but they do so with reference to the past. So much of John's theology and symbolism is shaped by the Hebrew Bible. While he doesn't often quote the Hebrew Bible, almost every verse of Revelation is steeped in its traditions. This is a reminder for us that we need to know our history in order to know our future. John reveals that the God who created the world and called a covenant people will recreate the world and call all the nations to stream through its open gates. The God that is revealed is consistent, faithful, just, and watchful.

To live with hope is not to live without despair—they are two sides of the same coin. Indeed, hope is required precisely in moments of despair when we feel utterly powerless to change our fate. We don't need hope when life is going wonderfully well! Perhaps that is why this text has particular appeal for those who know oppression all too well. It is a text for those who are in the minority, for those who feel powerless and face overwhelming injustice every day. The hope that God will act is not an excuse for inaction in the present: this hope fosters courage to act and to resist systems of evil and oppression in anticipation of God's new world.

Apocalyptic hope is hope that God will break into this world and recreate it as it was intended to be—a world where all the nations live together in harmony and where all can equally enjoy the fruit in the garden of God. This promise of hope and renewal is not just for the Christian community. John's vision of the End is expansive. For any reader who is discouraged, disempowered, or struggling to flourish, Revelation's visions offer a glimpse of a world where all have access to healing, sunlight, water, and peace, and where Death and evil have lost their power.

I leave the final word to John who writes in 22:17:

> *"Come. Let anyone who wishes take the water of life as a gift."*

Things for Normal People to Read (Or Not ... No Judgment)

General Books on Revelation

Darden, Lynne St Clair. *Scriptualizing Revelation: An African American Postcolonial Reading of Empire.* Atlanta, GA: SBL Press, 2015.

deSilva, David Arthur. *Discovering Revelation.* London: SPCK, 2021

Frilingos, Christopher A. *Spectacles of Empire: Monsters, Martyrs, and the Book of Revelation.* Philadelphia, PA: University of Pennsylvania Press, 2004.

Howard-Brook, Wes, and Anthony Gwyther. *Unveiling Empire: Reading Revelation Then and Now.* The Bible & Liberation Series. Maryknoll, NY: Orbis Books, 1999.

Koester, Craig R. *Revelation and the End of All Things.* Grand Rapids, Mich: Eerdmans Publishing, 2018.

Commentaries[1]

Blount, Brian K. *Revelation: A Commentary.* New Testament Library. Louisville, KY: Westminster John Knox Press, 2009.

Boring, M. Eugene. *Revelation.* Louisville, KY: Westminster John Knox Press, 1989.

Huber, Lynn R. *Revelation.* Wisdom Commentary. Collegeville, MN: Liturgical Press, 2023

Koester, Craig R. *Revelation: A New Translation with Introduction and Commentary.* Anchor Bible. New Haven, CT: Yale University Press, 2014.

Schüssler Fiorenza, Elisabeth. *Revelation: Vision of a Just World.* Minneapolis, MN: Fortress Press, 1991.

Books on Ancient Apocalyptic Literature Beyond Revelation

Carey, Greg. *Apocalyptic Literature in the New Testament.* Core Biblical Studies. Nashville, TN: Abingdon, 2016.

Carey, Greg. *Ultimate Things: An Introduction to Jewish and Christian Apocalyptic Literature.* St. Louis, MO: Chalice Press, 2005

Portier-Young, Anathea. *Apocalypse against Empire: Theologies of Resistance in Early Judaism.* Grand Rapids, MI: W.B. Eerdmans Pub. Co, 2011.

---

[1] There are tons of excellent commentaries on Revelation so this is a very small selection that represents a range of views.

Acknowledgments

I was delighted to receive an invitation to write for *The Bible for Normal People* series as I have been a fan of their books and podcast for years. Thanks to Pete Enns and Jared Byas for their trust in me. I knew of them long before they knew of me, but I hope this book is a worthy addition to the really important work they are doing in trying to "ruin" the Bible for people!

A massive thanks go to Lauren O'Connell and Caroline Blyth whose questions, comments, corrections, and insights were invaluable. You are both extraordinary editors who have improved my writing, saved me from embarrassing errors, and helped me clarify my thoughts. Thank you.

I have been fortunate to have colleagues and students with whom I have discussed Revelation over years and whose work continues to shape and challenge my own. Several of these colleagues are cited in the book or recommended in the reading list and I am in their intellectual debt.

Finally, thanks always to my ever supportive husband, Peter. I could not do what I do without your care for me and confidence in me.

About this Book

About the Author

Robyn Whitaker (PhD, University of Chicago Divinity School) is a New Testament scholar who has had a long fascination with John's Apocalypse. She is an ordained minister of the Uniting Church in Australia who lives in Melbourne, Australia with her husband and two retrievers. When she is not thinking about the Bible she likes to bake, hike, do yoga, and go to the beach. She is Associate Professor of New Testament at Pilgrim Theological College in the University of Divinity. You can find more of her writing at robynwhitaker.com

Behind the Scenes

Publishing Director Lauren O'Connell
Editor Caroline Blyth
Cover Design Danny Wong
Layout Designer Ania Lenihan

Special thanks to the eagle-eyed members of our Society of Normal People community who read through the final draft of the manuscript and provided feedback, caught spelling errors, and generally ensured we don't look like fools: Abraham A. Vidal, Dawn Campano Baker, Michael Burdge, Colin Connor, Anthony Hendriks, Scott Henwood, Brian Jones, Rebecca Ray, Clint Redwood, Peter Wall, Lynn Wallace, Katherine Wharton. We couldn't do what we do without you.

Enjoyed this Book?

Head over to thebiblefornormalpeople.com/join to join the Society of Normal People, where you can:

- access all of our classes and courses,
- connect with other "normal people,"
- enjoy sneak peaks into upcoming projects,
- have conversations with The Bible for Normal People team,
- *and* get podcast exclusives, including access to an ad-free stream.

Or follow us on Facebook and Instagram (@thebiblefornormalpeople) for more The Bible for Normal People content.

Made in United States
Orlando, FL
07 December 2023

40390495R00086